Cakes and Ale

Cakes and Ale

THE GOLDEN AGE OF BRITISH FEASTING

Judy Spours

the national archives

For O.B.K., and J.S.K.

First published in Great Britain in 2006 by
The National Archives
Kew, Richmond
Surrey, TW9 4DU, UK
www.nationalarchives.gov.uk

The National Archives (TNA) was formed
when the Public Record Office (PRO)
and Historical Manuscripts Commission (HMC)
combined in April 2003.

A CIP catalogue record for this book is available
from the British Library.

ISBN 1 905615 02 7
    978 1 905615 02 5

Page design and typesetting by KEN WILSON | POINT 918

Printed in the UK by BUTLER AND TANNER, FROME, SOMERSET

CONTENTS

INTRODUCTION THE VICTORIANS: TASTES FOR A NEW WORLD

*O*n May Day 1851 a glamorous crowd swept into London's Hyde Park, where a vast Crystal Palace, miraculously constructed of glass, opened its doors for the first time to select guests. It housed the Great Exhibition of the Works of Industry of All Nations, the innovative international exhibition of manufactured products, and the ambitious brainchild of Prince Albert and of Henry Cole of the Royal Society of Arts.

After deprivations and disciplines in the first half of the nineteenth century, a lighter but more determined mood was in the air – one of passionate belief in progress, and of curiosity, particularly about science, nature and art. It was just such mid-Victorian energy and willingness to experiment that underpinned the ambitious Great Exhibition, where close to 100,000 exhibits were seen, between May and October that year, by six million visitors. Some people may have visited more than once, but this staggering number still represented a fifth of Britain's total population at the time. This was the first must-see blockbuster exhibition. People came from all over the country on day trips, the journeys made possible to so many by the recent technology of railways. And it was not just the wealthy or middle class who made the trip: many less affluent people also travelled up to London, sometimes subsidized in part by their masters in order that they, too, could see the progressive wonders on display.

And the exhibits were extraordinary to the mid-Victorian visitor. There were wonderful examples of new technology, including a gadget that could lift a patient from a hospital bed so that it could be made up under him,

Opposite *Inside the Crystal Palace at the Great Exhibition of 1851 an elegant group, some taking refreshments, are gathered under two of Hyde Park's trees contained within the structure. This painting by Louis Haghe gives a strong impression of the scale and atmosphere of the Palace, with its tiers of exhibition space and its airy grandeur.*

8

the latest in false teeth and artificial limbs, Russian clocks, a forty-foot model of the new Liverpool docks, a plethora of domestic labour-saving devices, particularly for the kitchen, and modern tableware made by the newly invented technique of electroplating. Two great crowd pullers were the huge and inestimably valuable Koh-i-Noor diamond, which had been recently handed over as a 'gift' to Queen Victoria by the Sikh nation in the Punjab, and the towering stuffed Indian elephant nearby. There were also preserved foods: imported cocoa, coffee and tea; biscuits, lemonade and confectionery; cod liver oil from Newfoundland; fruit and nuts from the West Indies; Swiss chocolate and preserved meats. In the Chinese section there was an edible bird's nest, the basis for the soup. All this was on display in the glimmering Crystal Palace, designed by Joseph Paxton as a giant

The exhibits shown here on a top tier of the Crystal Palace are produce from Trinidad, the Bahamas and the Eastern Archipelago. The exotic foods displayed would have been unfamiliar to many of the Exhibition's visitors.

glasshouse on a scale never seen before. A magnificent fountain sent jets of water into the air, and the glass structure enclosed a number of mature trees of the park. Even sophisticate Charles Dickens was knocked sideways by the Exhibition, not knowing quite where to start in viewing the exhibits and hating the crowds, complaining that they were driving him out of London to the seaside for the summer.

Of course, all these visitors needed food and drink during their day trips to the Exhibition. The Royal Commission that had been set up as an organizing body, drawing on members from all walks of life (although not the labouring poor), had decided, first and foremost, that the refreshments on offer should not include any kind of alcoholic beverage. The anxiety was that the lower classes in particular, on such a special day out, would

The Drunkard's Children of 1848 by George Cruikshank caricatures prevalent mid-nineteenth-century anxieties about the dissolute behaviour of ordinary people. The scene takes place at a gin palace, where both adults and children are imbibing while babies are neglected.

NO LUNCHEON OR DINNER TABLE COMPLETE WITHOUT

H.D.RAWLINGS'

SODA POTASS

SELTZER WATERS

& Ginger Ale.

ABSOLUTELY PURE

Seltzer water, or soda water, was a popular mid-nineteenth-century drink, as were ginger ale and ginger beer. Visitors to the Great Exhibition could buy such beverages in the Crystal Palace, but the organizers had taken the decision to ban the sale of alcoholic drinks.

A street seller of baked potatoes, drawn in 1849, was one of thousands of such traders in British cities. His potatoes are pre-cooked at the baker's and kept hot on the street in a metal potato-can: the fire-pot suspended beneath the can heats a water boiler.

inevitably get drunk and that some sort of uncontrollable mayhem would ensue. This would never do in a situation where great masses of different social classes were gathered together for the first time to witness the uplifting exhibits. Observers had already recorded what they deemed unacceptable behaviour in the lower classes on their days out to fairs on high days and holidays, such as those at Greenwich outside London or Donnybrook in Dublin, which one commentator described as 'a kind of popular festival' at which there is 'wild tumult'. The agricultural classes were seen to be particularly at fault, drinking beer, strong ale, cider and spirits – sometimes mixed together – to excess. This resulted in 'pernicious effects … on the habits, morals, families and dependents' of the drinkers, and numbers of such suspicious characters would be coming up to London. The Great Exhibition was designed to be a place of worthy, instructional entertainment and a demonstration of the successes of the age, not a riotous day out; only good-humoured and orderly pleasure was required.

More than a million bottles of non-alcoholic drinks were sold in the Crystal Palace during the five-and-a-half-month run of the Great Exhibition – lemonade, soda water, ginger beer, pear syrup – and these and other foodstuffs were chilled with 363 tons of 'rough ice'. Refreshments were served in various different eating areas. A tearoom served ices, frozen by a newfangled steam-driven refrigerator, sandwiches, pastries and patties,

12 and offered tea, coffee and cocoa alongside the other non-alcoholic drinks. Elsewhere you could buy bread and butter and cheese, buns and sausage rolls, pies and biscuits. Huge quantities of this fare were sold throughout the run of the Exhibition – 2,000 pineapples, 1,046 gallons of pickles, 2,400 quarts of jellies, for example – but nevertheless many visitors on their day out were not impressed with the quality and variety of this food. It had none of the exoticism of the preserved foods on display and it was expensive. Gradually, word got around about the unimaginative in-house catering and when it became clear that there was nothing in the rules of entry to the Exhibition that forbad the bringing in of food to the Palace, many cannier visitors brought their own picnics. An added

attraction of this self-help method of refreshment was that there was nothing to stop visitors bringing in alcoholic drinks either, so that jollier meals were laid out on the ground beside exhibits and glasses were raised in celebration.

One of the intentions of the Great Exhibition had been the lowering of social barriers by bringing all classes together in a common pursuit. But with the integration also came segregation. Fashionable society came to the Exhibition to see and be seen, not necessarily to be improved by exposure to the exhibits or to their less fortunate or affluent fellow countrymen and women. The fashionable also needed somewhere to eat in style, somewhere more appetizing than the offerings of the Crystal Palace. The great

*Two illustrations contrast social engagements. The delivery of a large, steaming bowl of punch to a party of men in a modest inn (**above**) was drawn in 1845. A genteel tea party in a High Victorian conservatory (**opposite**) was the front-page image of an 1881 edition of The Illustrated London News.*

14

An advertisement for a London-brewed beer emphasizes its purity and its modern production at a time when the quality of the drink varied widely. Beer might be watered down or otherwise adulterated to stretch out the quantity and increase the seller's returns.

LONDON LABOUR AND THE LONDON POOR.   97

THE IRISH STREET-SELLER.

This Irish street seller of oranges illustrated an edition of Henry Mayhew's groundbreaking survey London Labour and the London Poor, *first published in 1851. Mayhew detailed the work and lifestyles of the thousands of London street traders in food and drink.*

chef Alexis Soyer, who arrived in Britain from France in the 1830s and was chef of the Reform Club from 1837 to 1850, saw a culinary and business opportunity. Soyer leased Gore House, a mansion on the site of the present Albert Hall, and opened there an international restaurant, 'Soyer's Universal Symposium to All Nations', with a banqueting room that could accommodate 1,500 diners. In this elaborately decorated room he served continental – predominantly French – menus to the mainly British visitors, introducing many to new tastes for the first time. His ambition was to serve 5,000 meals a day, with differently priced menus for different pockets. But although many did take the opportunity to eat there, this catering enterprise also fell short of its ambitions and, by October, Soyer had closed his restaurant having made a staggering loss of £7,000 – about half a million pounds in today's terms.

Soyer was a modernizer, a celebrity chef but one who employed new kitchen technologies and organization of staff and food preparation, and who possessed a crusading determination to adjust the parlous state of the diets of the British. In 1847, at the Lord Lieutenant's request, he had taken his model soup kitchen to Ireland during the potato famine; and in 1855 he left for the Crimea at his own expense, vastly improving the diets of the soldiers serving there with the help of a new field stove that revolutionized army catering. He published several influential cookery books intended for a wide audience, such as *The Modern Housewife* in 1849 and *A Shilling Cookery for the People* in 1855.

In Britain the 1850s were a turbulent period of unprecedented social, economic and political changes and contrasts. Increasing numbers of newly affluent, newly middle-class Britons were gorging themselves, yet Oliver Twists, as revealed by Dickens in 1837–9, were still being reduced to pleading for another bowl of gruel. Feast or famine was the backdrop to a nation getting to grips with a new urbanization built on manufactured goods and their markets, a progress that was generous and cruel by turns, depending on the place occupied in the labour and social hierarchies. Those who were able to capitalize on the potential of the industrial age were keen to create an identity – through the way they lived, where they lived and very much through the way they ate and drank – that was visibly distinct from those beneath them in the social strata.

Class fluidity offered all the opportunities of a heady rise in the scheme of things, but it also presented an ever-present threat of falling back down. In such a social climate, appearances were felt to be vital, particularly if you were not quite as grand as you tried to be, and so the growing numbers of the middle class expended much energy on presenting themselves in the right light. This was an edgy game, sometimes resulting in pretensions that were wonderful material for satire. In his novel *Our Mutual Friend*, for example, published 1864–5, Dickens introduces 'Hamilton Veneering, Esquire, M.P. for Pocket-Breaches' and his wife, quintessential caricatures of the new middle classes with their polish not yet dry:

> Mr and Mrs Veneering were bran-new people in a bran-new house in a bran-new quarter of London. Everything about the Veneerings was spick and span new. All their furniture was new, all their friends were new, all their servants were new, their plate was new, their carriage was new, their harness was new, their horses were new, their pictures were new, they themselves were new, they were as newly married as was lawfully compatible with their having a bran-new baby, and if they had set up a great-grandfather, he would have come home in matting from the Pantechnicon,

Isabella Beeton's Book of Household Management *went through many editions after its first publication in 1861. This illustration for supper dishes, typically reliant on meat and fish, is taken from an 1888 edition, which contained additions to and variations from her original text.*

Roast Fowl.

Pheasant.

Game Pie with Jelly.

Shrimp Patties.

Oyster Patties.

Lobster Salad.

Savoury Jelly a la Bellevue.

Brawn.

Pigeon Pie.

Galantine of Veal.

Russian Salad.

Crayfish.

Ham Garnished.

Tongue Garnished.

without a scratch upon him, French polished to the crown of his head.

For, in the Veneering establishment, from the hall-chairs with the new coat of arms, to the grand pianoforte with the new action, and upstairs again to the new fire-escape, all things were in a state of high varnish and polish. And what was observable in the furniture, was observable in the Veneerings—the surface smelt a little too much of the workshop and was a trifle sticky.

In the chapters that follow, the likes of the Veneerings – the new suburban middle-class family – provide a fascinating starting-point for an exploration of British eating and drinking between the 1850s and the 1900s. The ways in which Victorians ate, drank and made merry are captured at home in family settings and when entertaining their guests; when at work and in the streets of the expanding industrial cities; in shrinking rural communities; and as they embarked on excursions, attended parties and took days off. Finally, in the early twentieth century, the last extravagances of the Edwardian social scene – its grand and conspicuous dining – are revealed, before the gourmet party ends with different obsessions in 1914.

*T*he burgeoning middle classes of the mid-nineteenth century, fortunate recipients of a new prosperity built on manufacturing, marked themselves out from those below them in the social pecking order by their apparent respectability. The bedrock of this respectability was cemented behind closed doors, in the home. Here there was intended to be domestic order and genteel manners, although in fact there was some confusion about how these were to be successfully achieved. The new members of this class were not necessarily well educated; they were proud new entrepreneurs and professionals but nevertheless materialistic; they were ambitious, progressive, competent, but in many ways amateurs at the art of living well. Their confidence, although not easily undermined, could teeter off balance in their attempts to get things right.

Lifestyle advice was soon to be on hand, though, for these occupants of newly built villas, which from the 1850s onwards were likely to be located in the suburbs rather than in the noisy and chaotic inner cities. From London, for example, the rich moved out to Barnes or Richmond. The more affluent middle classes might be found in Hampstead or Ealing, and the lower middle classes in Camberwell or Leyton. In his *Handbook to the Environs of London*, James Thorne describes such established suburbs. (Between the Great Exhibition of 1851 and publication of Thorne's book in 1876, the British middle class had tripled in size.) Barnes, for example, 'has

An 1892 edition of Mrs Beeton's Book of Household Management *illustrates fashionable breakfast tablewares. Some, with their oriental motifs and forms, are in a long-popular chinoiserie style; others are in keeping with the ubiquitous Victorian passion for floral decoration.*

20 lost much of its rural character by the inroads of the builder, and has nearly doubled in population during the last ten or twelve years.' Ealing village is 'lined with houses old and new, patches of greensward, gardens, shops, inns, and chapels, very irregular, in parts very picturesque'. In Leyton, 'As elsewhere the fields have been much encroached on; but much land is still under culture as market gardens and nursery grounds, and large quantities of roots and flowers are grown for Covent Garden market.' It was, though, a place 'formerly ... the residence of many great City merchants, and other wealthy personages. These have mostly retreated farther from the capital...', demonstrating that the top layer of the middle class was equally determined to separate itself from the threat of the parvenus below as they themselves were to stay distinctly above the labouring classes.

How to live well

The help needed for the recently middle class to create suitable living styles and manners came in the form of a boom in domestic how-to magazine articles and books, gratefully devoured by the new suburbanites. These publications offered advice on how to decorate and furnish the home; how to organize family life; how to choose, buy and cook food for family meals and dinner parties; even how to arrange the tablewares and decorations of the dining table. They dictated correct manners and also suggested methods with which to inspire or control them in others, particularly the servants who were now on the list of middle-class acquisitions, often for the first time.

Eliza Acton first published her *Modern Cookery for Private Families* in 1845, revising the text in 1855, and the book remained in print throughout the nineteenth century and on until 1914. Acton dedicated it to 'the Young

An illustration from Mrs Beeton shows a wide range of the preserved foods that could stock a Victorian larder, including dried and bottled fruits, cured and tinned meats – such as ham, salt beef and tongue – and kippered fish.

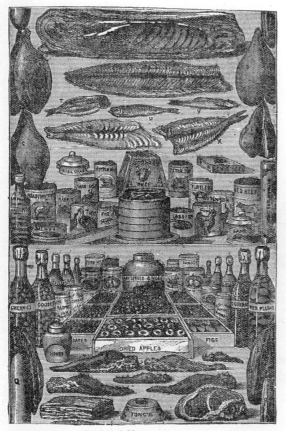

Preserved Meats, etc.

a. Side of Bacon ; *b.* York Ham ; *c.* Irish Ham ; *d.* Canadian Ham in bag ; *e.* Bath Chaps ;
f. Hung Beef ; *g.* Salt Beef ; *h.* Pressed Beef ; *i.* Ox Tongue ; *k.* Russian Tongue ; *l.* Pickled
Tongue ; *m.* Smoked Tongue ; *n.* Reindeer Tongue ; *o.* Sheep's Tongue ; *p.* German
Sausage ; *q.* Bologna Sausage ; *r.* Turtle (dried) ; *s.* Kippered Salmon ; *t.* Kippered Herring ;
u. Smoked Herring ; *v.* Yarmouth Bloater ; *w.* Salt Cod ; *x.* Finnan Haddock ; *y.* Ringed Dish

Housekeepers of England', for whom it was to
be a valuable guide, with its well-written and
well-observed recipes. It was wonderfully up-to-
the-minute, taking account of contemporary
kitchen technology and presenting recipes in a
tried and tested, discursive way, with a précis of
the essential ingredients, cooking times and
methods, as we would recognize them today but
new at the time. Acton's book makes use of new
preserved foodstuffs that could be bought in grocers' shops of the period – preserves and bottled
sauces, for example. Harvey's bottle sauce, she
says, is one of the earliest, similar to Chinese soy
sauce with its dark colour and sharp taste, but
she notes that Worcester sauce has come to
replace it. Many of her recipes sound delicious
and inventive, written with the encouraging zeal
of someone who really liked her food. Her complicated recipes for quince blancmange, for
instance, might be readily embarked on by cooks
eager to capture the effect on the taste buds she
describes: 'This, if carefully made, and with ripe
quinces, is one of the most richly-flavoured
preparations of fruit that we have ever tasted;
and the receipt, we may venture to say, will be
altogether new to the reader.' Perhaps the blancmange would be eaten with her delicious salad
of mixed summer fruits: strawberries, white and

21

red currants, white or red raspberries, with sifted sugar and two glasses of Madeira, sherry or good white wine.

Acton was born in Suffolk, but later lived in Hampstead – the sort of middle-middle-class suburb that would have been home to many of her readers, making her an ideal mentor. The serious message of her approach to cooking was a concern for proper diet, first and foremost that of the man of the family, whom she considered needed and deserved to be well fed because his industry in art, literature or science was achieving advancements that were to the benefit of civilization. Home-cooked food should, therefore, be wholesome in order to promote, not injure, health. She advises the use of fresh local ingredients for recipes that were mostly English, although her section on foreign cookery includes Jewish recipes and dishes from France, Mauritius, India, Italy, Germany, Switzerland, Austria and the Arab world. There is, for example, a Jewish almond pudding, Indian Burdwan (a chicken dish), the King of Oude's omlette recipe, Turkish and Arabian pilaws, Milanese risotto, German broiled eels with sage, and 'Kedgeree or Kidgeree, an Indian breakfast dish'. A shrimp chatney [sic] recipe comes from Mauritius, another from Bengal; French recipes are scattered throughout the book, for pastry mixes, soufflés and fondues. This was an excellent book, which rival authors and publishers were keen to plunder, so that by the 1861 edition Acton complained in the text about plagiarism of her work by 'strangers coolly taking the credit and the profits of my toil'.

One fount of advice more famous still today who cannot be said to be totally innocent of the crime of plundering Acton's work is Mrs Beeton. Her *Book of Household Management* first appeared in volume form in 1861, although its publication in monthly parts began in 1859. Both Eliza Acton and Isabella Beeton have been widely imagined as rosy-cheeked, middle-

Imported preserved foods, such as desiccated (dried) coconut, presented the late Victorian housewife with an opportunity to extend her range of baking and pudding-making. In this advertisement it was deemed necessary to display the originating coconut to explain the product.

aged housewives, but the image does not fit the facts. Acton never married, adopting the rather risqué female profession of writer of poetry and newspaper articles, and lived much of her life with her mother. Beeton was only twenty-five when her book was published in 1861, the young wife of imaginative publisher Samuel Beeton – and she died at twenty-eight of puerperal fever after giving birth to her fourth child.

Since the early years of her marriage, Mrs Beeton had been contributing to her husband's *Englishwoman's Domestic Magazine*, and the starting-point for *Household Management* was as a compendium spin-off of the magazine. It was an ambitious work, resolutely didactic but with a charm and youthful earnestness that relieve the rigour of Beeton's cause to promote solid, reliable domestic values and harmony for the middle class. 'I have always thought,' she writes in her Preface, 'that there is no more fruitful source of family discontent than a housewife's badly-cooked dinners and untidy ways.' The book's recipes and its careful instruction on the duties of the mistress of the house and her staff – from Housekeeper to Cook and Butler to lowly Maid-of-all-Work – and on the 'uses of all things connected with home life and comfort' made it a brilliantly commercial bible of respectability rules for the middle-class housewife. It cleverly sets out to span the breadth of this market in, for example, its ambiguous descriptions of the role of the housekeeper, who might in fact be one and the same as the mistress in the less affluent of the households within its commercial range. Beeton's text at times subtly glamorizes the housekeeper's role so that a reader with few servants to her name would not feel undermined if there was a little do-it-herself going on:

> As a rule, it may be stated, that the housekeeper, in those establishments
> where there is no house steward or man cook, undertakes the preparation of
> the confectionary [*sic*], attends to the preserving and pickling of fruits and

Mrs Beeton made no assumptions about the prior housekeeping knowledge of her readers, as this annotated illustration of basic fruits demonstrates. Pineapple had been a prized delicacy, and a symbol of affluence, since the late seventeenth century as it was complicated and expensive to cultivate it in a British climate.

1.—Black Grapes. 2.—Muscat Grapes. 3.—Tangerines. 4.—Bananas. 5.—Oranges.
6.—Peaches. 7.—Pears. 8.—Pineapple. 9 and 10.—Apples.

vegetables; and, in a general way, to the more difficult branches of the art of cookery.

The instructions Beeton gives for every domestic detail are minute, and by today's fashions can appear intimidating and regimented. 'When the dinner hour has arrived,' she says, '…then comes haste; but there must be no hurry—all must work with order.' Later, she expands on the necessity of this approach: 'The nation which knows how to dine has learnt the leading lesson of progress. It implies both the will and the grace to reduce to order.' And order was one of the hallmarks of that desired respectability.

The recipes themselves, of course, give some insight into mid-Victorian eating patterns, although the picture gained is as precarious as it would be today if we tried to draw conclusions about someone's diet from the cookery books on their shelves rather than from their supermarket receipts. Because you read *How to Be a Domestic Goddess* does not mean that you are one, and the same was true in the nineteenth century. But Mrs Beeton's *Household Management* does provide a fascinating piece of the history of how people liked to be *seen* to cook and eat. A striking difference between now and then is that we may be left bemused by elaborate recipes presented to us in books today, and wonder how they are

26

going to hang together, whereas Mrs Beeton knew she was starting from zero and left little to chance. In her book you can have detailed instruction, including the cost of ingredients and whether appropriate to the season of the year, for making a cheese sandwich or boiling a potato. Even now such advice is often useful and many of her recipes are ones that we still make. This may be particularly the case with the sort of classically English recipes that are passed down from generation to generation, for Orange Marmalade or for 'An Unrivalled Plum-Pudding' on Christmas Day, for example; or for Seed-cake or Scotch Shortbread, Mint Sauce or Goose-berry Jam. Our great-great-grandmothers may have read the recipes in Mrs Beeton first, and they have become our own family versions with the passage of time. There are also recipes that are certainly not to our contemporary tastes or proprieties, such as Roast Larks, Minced Veal and Macaroni, and Turtle Soup, which would be unlikely to promote a desired domestic harmony in the twenty-first century.

The servant problem

Victorian domestic harmony was unlikely to reign, and the meals would not be cooked and served, unless there was concord with and among the servants of the household. In the 1850s there were over a million servants in Britain, working in households ranging from the aristocratic, which might employ hundreds, to the lower middle-class one of a clerk, who had to make do with one maid-of-all-work. Mrs Beeton outlines the duties of different servants, of a quantity that might be employed by a well-to-do middle-class family, and she takes care to indicate which duties might be taken on by others if the overall number of staff is smaller. The clear indications of individual responsibilities she gives may have greatly helped, for

28 if everyone knew what was expected of them there was less room for dispute. But she is as aware as her readers – some of whom were themselves, perhaps, at only one remove from the servant state in life – might be of the possible mistreatment of domestic staff, and is keen to distance a sensible, fair, middle-class employer from the proclivities of those further up the social scale. She opens her chapter 'Domestic Servants' thus:

> It is the custom of 'Society' to abuse its servants … matronly ladies, and ladies just entering on their probation in that honoured and honourable state … talk of servants, and, as we are told wax eloquent over the greatest plague in life while taking a quiet cup of tea.

Others, though, might have been unconvinced by Beeton's attempts to distance the middle class from bad behaviour towards servants. Indeed, many servants themselves thought they were likely to be treated less well in a middle-class household than in an aristocratic one, where they might expect to find at least a practised *noblesse oblige*. In 1847 two of the brothers Mayhew, Augustus Septimus and the more famous Henry, an originator of *Punch* magazine and later a powerfully philanthropic chronicler of the lives of London's poor, published *The Greatest Plague of Life: or the Adventures of a Lady in Search of a Good Servant*. Illustrated with parodic drawings by George Cruikshank, it purports to be written *by One Who Has Been "Almost Worried to Death"* and is the bleakly humorous tale of the world's worst employer,

A Satisfying Meal, *1883, by Charles Meer Webb, is a charmingly observed scene, down to the creases in the white damask tablecloth, the robust enjoyment of the elderly man, napkin tied round his neck, the attentive tabby cat – and a kindly, idealized housekeeper.*

An illustration by 'Phiz' to Charles Dickens' The Pickwick Papers of 1836–7 visualizes footman Mr Muzzle's kitchen. Sanctimonious servant Job Trotter encounters Sam Weller and other servants enjoying a hearty meal, empty bottles lining up beside a rather less than ideal housekeeper. The cat here is not so respectful as its counterpart opposite either, as it eyes up an extravagant supper opportunity.

Caroline, whose husband Edward is a lawyer – in the upper echelons of the middle class (they live in Regent's Park). Caroline is anything but the character she describes herself to be: '…weak, timid, and bashful as I was, (I have always been of a retiring disposition ever since I was a child)'. She tells tales of, for example, 'the terrible goings-on of my first maid, and whom we all expected would have turned out such a "treasure"…'. An argument starts with her cook, whom she suspects of theft: '…all of a sudden I missed a whole pound packet of Orange Pekoe Tea [a desirable import], which Edward had brought home from the City on purpose for me.' Then

The Greatest Plague of
Life *of 1847 by the Mayhew
brothers is a stinging comic
fiction about middle-class
attitudes towards house-
hold servants. George
Cruikshank's frontispiece
depicts the dreadful mistress
of the house, Caroline,
being 'nearly worried to
death' by her nightmare
servants who she imagines
here doing their neglectful
and destructive worst.*

there is one Mrs Yapp, a hypochondriacal servant who '…had gone raving mad about homeopathy, and had nearly starved herself to death with its finikin infinitessimal doses…' and 'that great, big, fat, overfed, stuck-up pig of a John Duffy of mine', who is treated with (un)righteous indignation:

> And, mercy-on-me! Even the common household bread wasn't good enough for his royal highness's delicate stomach! Ho no! he must needs go pampering himself with the digestive cottages I had expressly for myself of a morning. As for good wholesome salt butter, too, at one-and-one, I declare he wouldn't so much as soil his mouth with it; not he! But he'd wait till our butter-dish came down, and then *wouldn't* he fall at our fresh at one-and-eight, and spread it on a large bit of my digestive cottage—yes! As thick as stucco!

The passage illustrates a number of preoccupations of the age. The distinctions between the diets that could be expected by different classes are apparent, as is middle-class paranoia about the assumed perfidy of servants; and the gentility of new foods, such as Caroline's 'digestive cottage', is neatly highlighted; her servant should only expect rough brown bread. (But John Duffy could take retrospective delight in the possibility that Caroline could be slowly poisoned by her bread if it was adulterated by the addition of alum, an additive used by unscrupulous bakers to whiten its appearance.)

No one escapes Caroline's displeasure, not even a neighbour who is trying his hand at his own piece of admirable, but apparently doomed, domestic economy and right-thinking by cultivating fruit and vegetables when, in her opinion, all can be bought so cheaply at Covent Garden market that the activity is pointless. She mocks his attempts to 'force a cucumber or two' under a ground glass lampshade, saying that although he spent a fortune on manure, the only cucumber he produced was 'nipped in the

gherkin'. In fact, her neighbour was not alone in his efforts on the vegetable plot. Writing about the kitchen garden in *Home and Garden* of 1900, Gertrude Jekyll was extolling the virtues of cultivating vegetables of all branches of the cabbage and bean families. She recommended exotics such as Kohl-Rabi (a cabbage grown for its bulbous root, similar to turnip), sea kale, dandelions (popular in France, but never quite catching on in Britain, perhaps because of their other, folkloric associations), artichoke, endive, angelica, garlic and all manner of herbs – thyme, basil, tarragon, sage, balm, marjoram, borage, mint, bay and chervil. Some of her ideas would not look unusual in a cookery book today, but may not have been compelling to her audience of aspirant Victorians. 'A dish of dry Beans, soaked over-night, boiled and served with hot olive-oil poured over,' she explains, 'is the regular main meal of many a poor family in Southern Italy.'

Caroline's deep-rooted unpleasantness is lampooned in *The Greatest*

Plague of Life through her pretensions and hypocrisy – and her greed:

> I have always, ever since I was a child, made it a solemn duty to observe, with the greatest strictness, all the feasts which have been ordained by our venerable mother church. Thank goodness, I can lay my head on my pillow at night and safely say, that I have never allowed a single year to pass over my head without partaking with great devotion and extreme relish of the plum-pudding and mince-pie of Christmas, the pancake of Shrove Tuesday (by the bye, with a spoonful of gin, it eats just like ratafia, I can assure you) and the divine gooseberry tart of Easter Sunday; though, with all my enthusiasm, I can't say as much for that filthy salt cod of Ash Wednesday.

The delicacies eagerly consumed at some Victorian feasts are nicely described here, as is a suggestion of Caroline's tippling at the gin bottle, a weakness more usually described at the time from a pompous distance by middle class commentators on the shortcomings of the working classes. (Ratafia is both a brandy-based liqueur and an almond-flavoured biscuit or macaroon.) Caroline does get her comeuppance, however, in the conclusion of the book. Pointing out that she will never have a good servant because 'good mistresses make good servants' and, if treated well, servants and their employers will become good friends, Edward leaves her, dismisses the servants and sells off the household effects. In a more sombre summing up, he tells the readers that his society, the 'genteel world', is based on pride, vanity and show, and is one in which people's principal struggle is to trick their neighbours into believing that they are richer than they really are. This was a charge frequently levelled against the middle classes at the time from a variety of sources, each of whom – from social reformers to moral crusaders to nervous aristocrats – had reason to want them to keep their pretensions and their extravagances in check.

Good plain food

The potential for delicious meals to reward the man of the house and keep family life in happy order was enhanced by the increasingly wide range of foods available to those who could afford them – both basic ingredients and, as the century progressed, more and more preserved and processed foods.

Our middle-class housewife had to make regular purchases of perishable foods as only the most basic form of refrigeration was devised before the end of the century. Ice chests, consisting of a compartment in which to place block ice and another to hold the food, existed but would be most likely in grander households for storing perishables and for chilling ice creams and puddings for dinner parties. Many foods were delivered direct to the door – bread, meat, fish, fruit and vegetables. The butcher's boy might call in the morning, for example, to take the order for the day, returning later to deliver the meat. The supply of foods was more stable than it had been earlier in the century when it was reliant on the condition of domestic, British agriculture – home crop failures then meant lack of supply. The second half of the nineteenth century saw a massive increase in the importing of food, much of it from the New World, which also provided opportunities for the exotic. Fresh vegetables were grown in extensive market gardens in the suburbs, and were therefore readily available to those living nearby.

In *Household Management* Mrs Beeton arranges her suggestions for 'Plain Family

At the ring of the muffin man's bell, a maidservant runs up the steps from the kitchen of a Victorian terraced house, empty plate in hand, to buy breakfast for the household. Many fresh foods were purchased from traders soliciting custom in this way, or delivering orders.

"MUFFINS AND CRUMPETS!"

Dinners' by month of the year, appropriate to seasonal ingredients. A few examples give an idea of the menus eaten by a middle-class family (or which they hoped they might learn to cook and eat). For a Sunday in January she suggests boiled turbot with oyster sauce and potatoes; a roast leg or griskin (loin) of pork with apple sauce, broccoli and potatoes; followed by Cabinet pudding (a steamed pudding with dried fruits) and damson tart made with preserved damsons. For a Friday in July she suggests roast shoulder of mutton, onion sauce, peas and potatoes, followed by cherry tart and baked custard pudding. A rather more elaborate Thursday in September calls for brill and shrimp sauce; roast hare, gravy and redcurrant jelly; mutton cutlets and mashed potatoes; then scalloped oysters, instead of a pudding. (Oysters were a cheap food at this date. Later in the century, over-fishing meant that they became an expensive luxury.)

It is hard to imagine many households that would have adopted this last menu in its entirety for an everyday meal. And of course many everyday dishes were prepared without the aid of a cookery book, and were passed around by word of mouth. In *A London Girl of the 1880s* Molly Hughes remembers her mother's familiarity with the modern ideas of 'Domestic Economy' found in magazines and books, but recounts her less formal, and possibly less reliable, methods of disseminating domestic information, such as the recipe for a fine rice pudding:

> A dropper-in to lunch had enjoyed her pudding and began:
>
> 'How do you manage to get such good rice puddings, Mrs Thomas? My cook is so uncertain—one day we can swim in it, and the next day we can dance on it. Do tell me exactly how you get it just right like this.'
>
> 'You take a pie-dish.'
>
> 'What size?'
>
> 'Oh, the ordinary size. Put some well-washed rice in it.'
>
> 'How much?'
>
> 'Enough to cover the bottom. Then add a bit of butter.'
>
> 'How big a bit?'
>
> 'As big as a walnut. Then add salt and sugar.'
>
> 'How much?'
>
> 'Oh, as much as you think will do. Then bake in a very slow oven.'
>
> 'For how long?'
>
> 'Until it seems to be done.'

Those on lower budgets, in less genteel environments or in areas of the country within less easy reach of rail transportation feasted differently. In Scotland there might have been black pudding, sheep's head broth and a savoury trotter; or a tripe supper with a white onion sauce, and oysters and

ale. Visiting rural Wales, Molly Hughes observes the differences in diet, practicalities and food supply between the metropolis and the countryside:

> Butter and eggs could be obtained at uncertain intervals from a woman coming with a basket from a farm up among the hills. So uncertain were her visits that the butter had to be salted down in order to keep. There was no fruit to be had, no cake, and most astonishing to me for Wales, no cheese. There was no cool larder, and the heat was often so great that we could have frizzled bacon on the slate flags by the front door. Poultry was too dear to be considered. Bread was made at home by the servant, two vast loaves at a time, and carried down to a bake-house in the village.

To compile his 1855 *A Shilling Cookery for the People*, subtitled *Embracing*

38 *an entirely new system of plain cooking and domestic economy*, Alexis Soyer had, he says, left his 'fashionable culinary sanctorum' at the Reform Club to visit the homes of ordinary people, particularly in rural areas, to gain an understanding of their culinary lives. He finds that they have little idea how to cook, and Soyer undertakes to write recipes that will be of use 'to the artisan, mechanic, and cottager'.

The book opens with instructions for making stocks for soups, gravies and plain sauces, and continues in such logical and grass-roots style. Soyer includes a substantial section on 'What I Can Cook With My Gridiron', the simplest of cooking utensils.

> I use two kinds of gridirons, each costing very little; one is of cast iron, to go
> on the fire, and the other is of iron wire, made double, to hang from the bar
> of the grate before the fire, made so as not to too much press the object
> cooked within it.

In this basic way, many fish, he says, can be cooked – plain red herring, haddock, whitings, mackerel, flounders, soles, salmon, eels, ling – and meats. These include broiled or rump steak, mutton chop, veal cutlets, pork chops, calves' hearts, lamb chops, broiled ham, sausages, black pudding, kidneys, fowl and pigeons. Soyer also covers the favoured method of ordinary cooking at the time – in a frying pan. Apart from its general popularity, he feels 'the necessity of paying particular attention to it, as it is the utensil most in vogue in a bachelor's residence'. He does not presume to change such cooking habits, but to improve the contents of the pan. He discusses, for example, the finer points of frying a steak in a frying pan, and suggests seasonings such as the addition of chopped-up onions or shallots, parsley, mushrooms and pickles, to be fried at the same time. He demonstrates how to make a sauce by putting ingredients in the pan and heating them after the steak has been removed – pickled walnuts and gherkins,

Seville oranges, the basic ingredient for English marmalade, make so delicious-looking an artwork here that they are displayed on a plinth. Mrs Beeton gave three recipes for marmalade in her Book of Household Management, *adding the note that marmalade should be made in March or April, when the Seville oranges are 'in perfection'.*

oyster or mussel sauce, horseradish. Soyer also countenances the addition of bottled relishes and ketchups.

Soyer does voice some disapproval of the habit of the labouring classes of taking meat to the baker's to be cooked in his oven. Although this was seen as an economy, saving the purchase of fuel, or a necessity where cooking facilities were unavailable, Soyer is sceptical, suggesting that it is an act of laziness. The baker's oven, he says, is not equipped for the purpose of cooking meat dishes; some will be overcooked and some undercooked, and dishes were apt to get mixed up and people handed back something belonging to their neighbour. He is realistic enough, though, to know that he will not be able to reform 'this semi-barbarian method of spoiling food', and so provides instructions for doing it better, the principles of which endure to this day. He even provides a diagram of a superior arrangement of the dish in which the Sunday roast might be taken to the oven. A 'grating' with a trivet in the centre can be placed in the dish. The pudding (made with flour and suet) should then be placed at the bottom, potatoes placed on the grating and the joint of meat over the top on the trivet. Then fat from the meat will make the potatoes 'delicate and crisp'

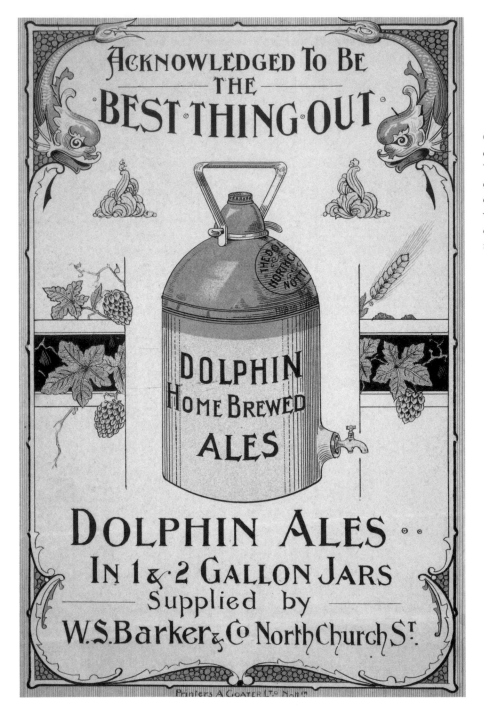

ACKNOWLEDGED TO BE
THE
·BEST·THING·OUT·

DOLPHIN
HOME BREWED
ALES

DOLPHIN ALES ··
IN 1 & ·2 GALLON JARS
Supplied by
W.S.Barker & Co North Church St.

Printers A Coater Ltd N.hm

Classical flourishes, including a frieze of hops, surround this 'home brewed' ale to give it a traditional, down-to-earth appeal. The large earthenware jar is sealed, has a strong carry-out handle and a tap to dispense the beer.

and will not fall into the pudding and prevent it from setting.

Soyer's *Shilling Cookery* is packed full of useful and down-to-earth advice, yet is combined with a Gallic touch that could only enhance the food on British tables. On the one hand, he points out that many cookery books will offer the middle class advice on how to choose the best joints of meat, but that his will give pointers about choosing second- and third-grade cuts of meat for the other two-thirds of the population. 'It is, therefore, our duty here to teach the labourer's and cottager's wife how to buy it [meat] cheap, sweet, wholesome, and nutritious.' On the other hand, in his discussion of refreshing, crisp salads, 'full of life and health', the Frenchman is revealed, and he gives a definitive simple recipe for a dressing for lettuce:

> Having cut it all up put it into a bowl; sprinkle over with your finger a small
> teaspoonful of salt, half one of pepper, three of oil, and two of English
> vinegar, or one of French; with the spoon and fork turn the salad lightly in
> the bowl till well mixed; the less it is handled the better; a teaspoonful of
> chopped chervil and one of tarragon is an immense improvement.

Convenience foods

A boon to the housewife or cook in the second half of the nineteenth century was the increasing availability of preserved, processed and packaged foods, which saved time and meant that a range of otherwise unobtainable ingredients could be readily at hand in the larder. Some had a significant effect on everyday menus, particularly on the parts that satisfied a sweet Victorian tooth. Packaged baking powder, a raising agent, opened up a much wider range of cake-baking and pudding-making; powdered gelatin enabled an everyday artistry in the towering and elaborate jellies that we associate with the Victorian dinner table. Jelly recipes were complicated,

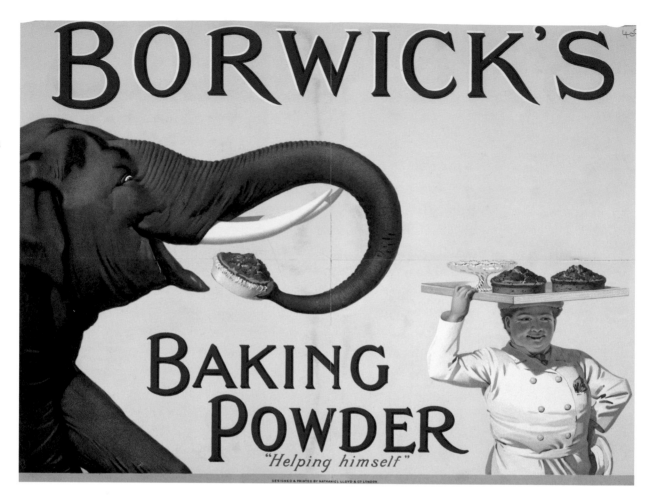

BORWICK'S

BAKING POWDER

"Helping himself"

DESIGNED & PRINTED BY NATHANIEL LLOYD & C? LONDON.

reliant on stock of calves' feet or cow heel, or 'isinglass' boiled, reduced and sieved through a cloth. Isinglass is a collagen obtained from the swimming bladder of certain fish that, when boiled, produces a pure form of gelatin. Soyer, for example, gives a number of recipes using these setting agents — for noyau, punch, orange, lemon, Madeira jellies — but is well aware of the time and effort required in their preparation. 'To those who wish to save trouble,' he suggests, 'I would recommend them to buy their jellies ready made. They may be purchased at almost every Italian warehouse in town and country, in bottles of about a pint and a quart each, so prepared as to keep fresh and good for years.'

The convenience of the new product baking powder meant it was no longer necessary to mix the raising agents required for many cakes and pies. Even less capable cooks could now bake with confidence.

The successful marketing of Bird's custard powder entailed an extensive and long-running advertising campaign. This advert appeared in The Illustrated London News *in 1886, proclaiming the great luxury of a powder that did away with the inconvenience of concocting custard from scratch.*

The arrival on the market of custard powder instantly demystified the uncertain art of creating real custard by heating milk and eggs, which had a tendency to curdle. The inventor of custard powder was pharmacist Alfred Bird, inspired by his wife's partiality to custard but constitutional intolerance to the eggs essential to the original dish. His powder was based on cornflower as an alternative thickening agent, and could be conveniently packaged and stored. Bird's success, though, was not just as an inventive chemist, but also as an astute entrepreneur. Bird's custard powder was marketed and advertised widely, achieving a level of distribution and prominence that successfully cornered the market.

One domestic anxiety was the freshness of milk before technology existed to keep it chilled in transport and in the larder. Even fresh milk, before pasteurization, posed significant and known health risks. It must have seemed something of a culinary miracle when, from the 1850s, canned condensed milk began to be imported into Britain from America and Switzerland. The heating process to condense the milk killed most of the harmful bacteria, and the addition of sugar to the product helped to prevent subsequent deterioration. The tinned, sweetened condensed milk tasted very different from fresh milk, but was thought delicious at the time (and well into the twentieth century), and was used in dessert, sweetmeat and baking recipes. Molly Hughes, working as a teacher in Darlington in 1886, remembers making comforting cups of cocoa with the aid of a spirit lamp and condensed milk. She would not have had access to fresh milk for the purpose in the dreary establishment in which she was working, and the delicious hot drink must have provided a fillip after the nightly supper she endured 'of baked potatoes … and *nothing* else at all'.

By the 1890s, the range of processed and packaged foods on offer to those with the resources to buy was substantial. Margarine was invented

44 in France in 1869, a mixture of oil from beef fat and skimmed milk and water; it became a successful and widely exported butter substitute. From the 1870s cheese was produced in factories in Britain, and later imported from America and Australia. Along the Thames in London, a food processing industry gathered pace in Lambeth, London Bridge and Bermondsey. Breweries produced beer and vinegar, flour was milled and factories concocted sauces and meat essences. From 1866 the pungent smells of beer brewing in the east of the city were mixed with the sweet and sickly odours of biscuit production at Peek Frean's factory. Here they produced 'Fine Navy Biscuits' for soldiers of the Franco-Prussian war of 1870, and the first ever chocolate biscuit, the 'Chocolate Table', in 1899. Pearce Duff manufactured blancmange powder, a cornflower-based product similar to custard powder, which eventually resulted in millions of pink blancmange rabbits at children's parties, through to the late twentieth century. Crosse & Blackwell, meanwhile, also at London Bridge, manufactured fruit chutneys and hot chilli pepper sauces in imitation of the recipes the British tasted in India. Bovril beef extract was invented by a Scotsman and developed by him in Canada before his return to Britain and the establishment of a factory in Farringdon Road in the late 1880s. Soon thousands of public houses and bars were selling hot Bovril, and the product in jars was on sale in grocers' shops.

Then there were dried vegetables and soups, tinned soups, bottled pickles, tinned meats (such as beef and tongue), tinned fish (such as salmon), factory produced jam, tinned fruits (such as peaches, apricots and pineapples from California) and, in the 1890s – from the factories of Heinz in

The Bovril beef extract that the mother here wants to add as stock to a stew she is making is so delicious that her little daughter is eating it by the spoonful. A toy bull on wheels reminds us of the origins of the product.

"Wherever did I put that BOVRIL!"

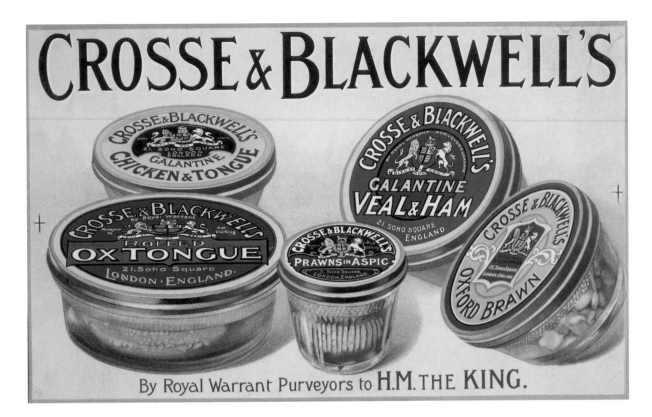

CROSSE & BLACKWELL'S

CHICKEN & TONGUE

GALANTINE VEAL & HAM

ROLLED OX TONGUE
21, Soho Square
LONDON · ENGLAND.

PRAWNS IN ASPIC

OXFORD BRAWN

By Royal Warrant Purveyors to H.M. THE KING.

An early twentieth-century advertisement for potted meats and seafood illustrates preserved products of the kind introduced in the mid-nineteenth century and which sold consistently through most of the twentieth. The faithful painting of the jars is sufficient to promote the foods.

Pittsburgh, Pennsylvania – baked beans in tomato sauce. Chocolate was manufactured by Fry's from the 1840s, Cadbury's created the first milk chocolate in Britain in the 1890s and in 1881 in York the Rowntree Cocoa, Chocolate & Chicory Works decided to produce fruit pastilles; they went on to pioneer chocolate drops, fruit gums and jelly babies.

New meals at new times

The men of the villas of Barnes or Hampstead or Ealing were able to live in such desirable suburbs because they could afford to travel by train into London to their professional or commercial places of work. Before they set out, a hearty breakfast was the order of the day. Along with the familiar rolls, toast and eggs, breakfast could also involve a number of cuts of meat, either hot or cold. Most important were copious cups of tea, a ritual the

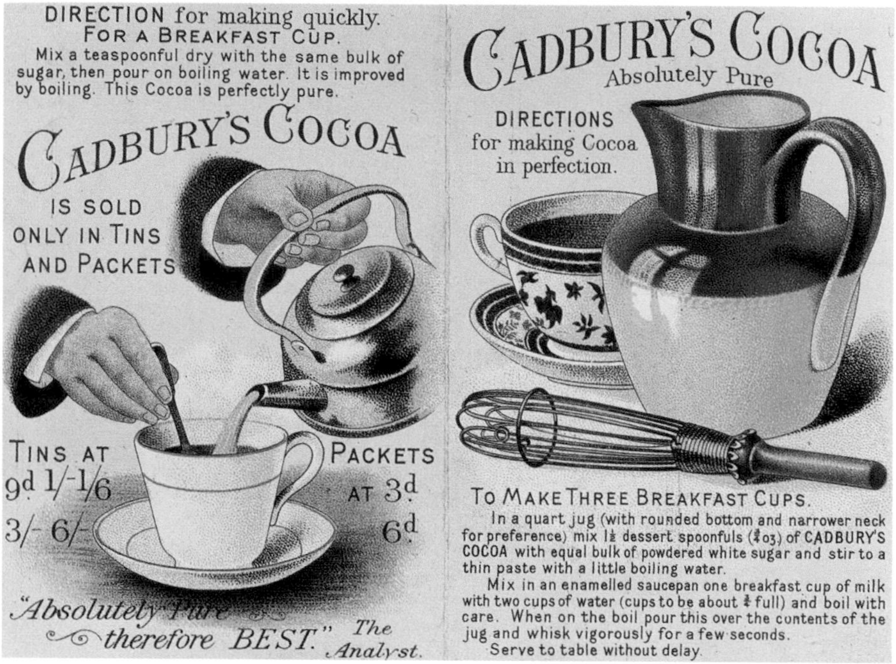
DIRECTION for making quickly.
FOR A BREAKFAST CUP.
Mix a teaspoonful dry with the same bulk of sugar, then pour on boiling water. It is improved by boiling. This Cocoa is perfectly pure.
CADBURY'S COCOA
IS SOLD ONLY IN TINS AND PACKETS
TINS AT 9d 1/-1/6 3/- 6/-
PACKETS AT 3d 6d
"Absolutely Pure therefore BEST." The Analyst.
CADBURY'S COCOA
Absolutely Pure
DIRECTIONS for making Cocoa in perfection.
TO MAKE THREE BREAKFAST CUPS.
In a quart jug (with rounded bottom and narrower neck for preference) mix 1½ dessert spoonfuls (¾ oz) of CADBURY'S COCOA with equal bulk of powdered white sugar and stir to a thin paste with a little boiling water.
Mix in an enamelled saucepan one breakfast cup of milk with two cups of water (cups to be about ¾ full) and boil with care. When on the boil pour this over the contents of the jug and whisk vigorously for a few seconds.
Serve to table without delay.

These detailed instructions for making a cup or a jug of Cadbury's cocoa demonstrate a need for explanations of the proper use of new packaged products. The recipes here are for the cocoa powder mixed with sugar and hot water; the addition of milk was not much in fashion until the twentieth century.

complexities of which Mrs Beeton refers to frequently when talking about servants' duties, for example those of the housemaid. Before she saw to the laying of the breakfast table, she had to organize the heating of the tea urn or the kettle on the kitchen fire, remove it to the parlour and then make sure that it was kept hot there.

Up in town, the working man would need to eat lunch in the middle of the day, a meal that might also provide business opportunities, or at least business gossip, with fellow diners. Depending on his pocket or his tastes, this meal might be taken at a restaurant, a coffee house, a public house, a dining house or a fashionable grill room. Railway inns, restaurants and refreshment rooms sprang up around major stations to accommodate and feed travellers. The possibilities on offer in restaurants are described by Tabitha Tickletooth, the pseudonymous author of *The Dinner Question or How to Dine Well and Economically* in 1860. She judges, for example, that the high reputation of Simpson's in the Strand is justified:

The charge is *two shillings*, for the joint, two kinds of vegetables, bread,

cheese, butter, and celery. Fish and soup may be added for another shilling, and a *few* well-composed made-dishes à la carte. This is par excellence the DINNER OF THE DAY. Its fare is purely English, and those who have once had a cut at its "saddles" or "surloins, turbot or salmon," never fail to come again.

In most establishments, meat was the dominant item on the menu: beef, mutton, pork, veal and ham. And of course along with the food went the drink, ales, wines and spirits. At all ends of the social scale drinking was in earnest. While much of the literature of the period about drinking habits has the *de haut en bas* tone of middle-class commentary on working-class enjoyments, William Thackeray enjoys caricaturing the wine-drinking antics of 'Club Snobs' in his *The Book of Snobs* of 1852:

I have remarked this excessive wine-amateurship especially in youth. Snoblings from College, Fledglings from the army, Goslings from the public schools, who ornament our Clubs, are frequently to be heard in great force upon wine questions. "This bottle's corked," says SNOBLING; and MR SLY,

48 the butler, taking it away, returns presently with the same wine in another jug, which the young amateur pronounces excellent.

The author claims that he himself belongs to nine clubs, all with suitable names, such as Sash and Marlingspike (military), Guy Fawkes (political), Brummell (dandy) and Acropolis (literary). He goes on to list the appalling drinking habits of young club snobs up in town from breakfast onwards, as they move from brandy and soda-water through wines to mulled port and, finally, to whisky punch with supper.

Back home in the respectable suburbs, new meal times and compositions were developed to accommodate the commercial day. The wife at home would generally take luncheon with the children, or she would eat alone, soup or a sandwich. And, because the hour of dinner was pushed back to eight or nine o'clock from five or six, a new meal was introduced – Tea. The

A WORD ABOUT DINNERS.

ENGLISH Society, my beloved Bob, has this eminent advantage over all other —that is, if there be any society left in the wretched distracted old European continent—that it is above all others a dinner-giving society. A people like the Germans, that dines habitually, and with what vast appetite I need not say, at one o'clock in the afternoon—like the Italians, that spends its evenings in opera-boxes— like the French, that amuses itself of nights with *eau sucrée* and intrigue— cannot, believe me, understand Society rightly. I love and admire my nation for its good sense, its manliness, its friendliness, its morality in the main—and these, I take it, are all expressed in that noble institution, the dinner.

The dinner is the happy end of the Briton's day. We work harder than the other nations of the earth. We do more, we live more in our time, than Frenchmen or Germans. Every great man amongst us likes his dinner, and takes to it kindly. I could mention the most august names of poets, statesmen, philosophers, historians, judges, and divines, who are great at the dinner-table as in the field, the closet, the senate, or the bench. Gibbon mentions that he wrote the first two volumes of his history whilst a placeman in London, lodging in St. James's, going to the House of Commons, to the Club, and to dinner every day. The man flourishes under that generous and robust regimen; the healthy energies of society are kept up by it; our friendly intercourse is maintained;

15   17

distinctions between, and social indications of, Afternoon Tea and High Tea warrant explanation. Afternoon Tea had been becoming fashionable since the late eighteenth century and, by the middle of the nineteenth,

This drop-initial, complete with appropriate snooty character, is from the opening page of a chapter of William Thackeray's The Book of Snobs, first published in 1852, in which the author dissects the snobberies rampant in British 'dinner-giving society'.

was established as a light meal of bread and butter, cake and fruit and, of course, tea. The meal filled the hunger gap between luncheon and the later dinner hour. High Tea was a much more substantial meal, established as a working-class main meal of the day. This was particularly the case in rural areas where the late afternoon or early evening would mark the end of the labourer's or agricultural worker's day and he and the rest of the family were all returned home. As a result, the nature of the meal called 'Tea' in a household marked social class.

Even then, High Tea itself involved subtle social distinctions depending on the fare on offer, and was further complicated by the fact that it might well also have been eaten in middle-class households on a Sunday. In the north of England and Scotland, High Tea was a hefty meal that included cooked fish or meat, probably fried in a pan, an important element if the working man had taken only a chunk of bread and an onion out with him to eat for lunch. A more genteel version, of the kind eaten across the class divide on Sundays, required the prettiest transfer-printed crockery, including tablewares specially designed for the purpose, such as cress drainers and crumpet or muffin dishes, which had hollow containers for hot water at the base and covers to keep the contents warm. Such a tea would have, for example, cold cuts such as ham or chicken, perhaps a meat pie, salad, crumpets, fruit bread, jams and cakes. Regional variations might dictate the inclusion of, say, oatcakes in Scotland and Welsh cakes in Wales.

But in the middle of a working week, High Tea was rarely eaten in the suburbs. The middle-class man, if he was fortunate, returned home to one of the terrifyingly meaty and elaborate 'Plain Dinners' of the kind suggested by Mrs Beeton, which he would enjoy with his family at a respectably late hour.

Decisions about everyday family meals as a constituent of a well-oiled family unit were as nothing, though, compared to the effort and anxiety required for successful entertaining at home. The Victorian middle classes entertained frequently, to nurture social relationships and business connections and to put on show their domestic achievements – or, put another way, their affluence relative to that of their chosen guests. It would not be unusual for a household to throw an average of one dinner party a week, which could be for a dozen guests offered as many as twenty or thirty dishes, prepared and served by a crew of domestic servants. A high proportion of income was expended in this way, as well as a high proportion of a housewife's energy.

The right stuff

Inviting people round meant that not only menus and the merits of the cook were on display, but the whole environment of the home. The interior decoration of the principal rooms, and the setting of the dinner table, made up a crucial part of the evening's demonstration. Questions of taste were of great interest to the self-improving Victorian, yet just what constituted good taste could be hard to fathom, and a challenge to adhere to.

This supper table design for sixteen is from an 1892 edition of Mrs Beeton. Cold dishes are presented on the table and plates are ready for guests to serve themselves. Three wine glasses are set at each place, one of coloured glass to indicate its use. The arrangement of upholstered bench seats makes it possible to accommodate the large number of diners.

The Victorian housewife gave serious consideration to questions of whether her home contained the right stuff. And often, certainly in the middle of the century, this meant a great deal of stuff, of a density and elaboration that is easy to find amusing today and which infuriated the design pundits of the day.

Once again, home-makers could take advantage of published advice, this time about good taste in home decoration – although they must sometimes have felt themselves at the mercy of the disapproving taste-makers. Pre-eminent among those who provided advice was Charles Eastlake. Trained as an architect but working as a designer, principally of furniture, Eastlake possessed strong, common-sense views about functional furnishings. He urged restraint, simplicity in design, despairing of the mid-nineteenth-century weakness for over-elaboration and pretentious display, which he and other critics had been pained to witness in many of the British displays of domestic design at the 1851 Great Exhibition. Eastlake published his influential *Hints on Household Taste* in 1868 and the book was republished many times during the rest of the century, becoming something of an interiors bible for the discerning.

In his fourth and revised edition of 1878, Eastlake states his case clearly: 'We can hardly hope then, in our own time, to sustain anything like a real and national interest in art while we tamely submit to ugliness in modern manufacture.' He then turns his attention to every detail of manufactured goods for the home, assessing their strengths, and more often their weaknesses, in functionality and appearance. He is unequivocal about the importance of design for dining:

> A well-appointed dinner-table is one of the triumphs of an English
> housewife's domestic care. That the cloth shall be of fine and snow-white
> damask; that the decanters and wine-glasses shall be delicate in form and of

Henry Cole's mid-century painting The Dinner Party *focuses on a beautiful young woman looking off to the side of the room: she may be waiting for her food to arrive or perhaps have some other story to tell. Meanwhile, gentleman and footman concentrate on the dispensing of fine wines.*

purest quality; that the silver shall look as bright and spotless as when it first came wrapped in tissue-paper from the silversmith's; that the épergne shall be filled with choicest flowers—these are points which she will consider of as much importance as the dainty skill of the cook's art itself.

True to his mantra of simplicity and restraint, Eastlake provides guidelines about the choice of dining table and chairs, of glass and ceramic and silver tableware, of cutlery and all possible accoutrements of dining. Tablewares are a particular source of frustration as, he says, 'there is no branch of art-manufacture exposed to greater dangers, in point of taste, than that of

These light and pretty table settings for a supper (**left**), perhaps at a musical evening or a ball, are characteristic of the less ornate styles that became established towards the end of the nineteenth century. There is something playful and rural in the bordered tablecloths and the bright little flowers, less ponderous than earlier Victorian tastes.

ceramic design'. Eastlake's hackles rise most readily when considering inappropriate ceramic shapes and decoration. 'A simple ring or round knob would be an infinitely better handle for dish-covers, &c., than the twisted stalks, gilt acorns, sea-shells, and other silly inventions,' he opines. 'As for the butter-cooler, it is, of course, surmounted by that inevitable cow which fashion has consecrated for our breakfast tables, in order, I presume, that we may never forget the source and origin of one of the most useful articles of daily food.' And the fashion for bright new chemical colours does not accord with Eastlake's more ascetic tastes:

> The *quality* of colour applied in the decoration of modern china is generally bad. Your pinks, mauves, magentas, and other hues of the same kind, however charming they may appear in the eyes of a court-milliner, are ignoble and offensive to the taste of a real artist, and are rendered more so in our porcelain by the fact of their being laid on in perfectly flat and even tints. It has been truly said that all noble colour, whether in pictorial or decorative art, will be found *gradated*, and on this point Nature herself may be quoted as a supreme authority.

Eastlake's design vision, with its fusion of a harking back to the solid designs of medieval craftsmen and a trumpeting of a modernism that would be

Desirable knives and forks (**opposite**), fit to grace an elegant dinner table, are depicted in a late nineteenth-century trade catalogue. Not before time, according to Charles Eastlake, writing in his Hints on Household Taste of 1868, '… the shape of an English dinner-knife, with its flat bone handle and straight, round-topped blade, is one of the most uninteresting that could be devised for the purpose.'

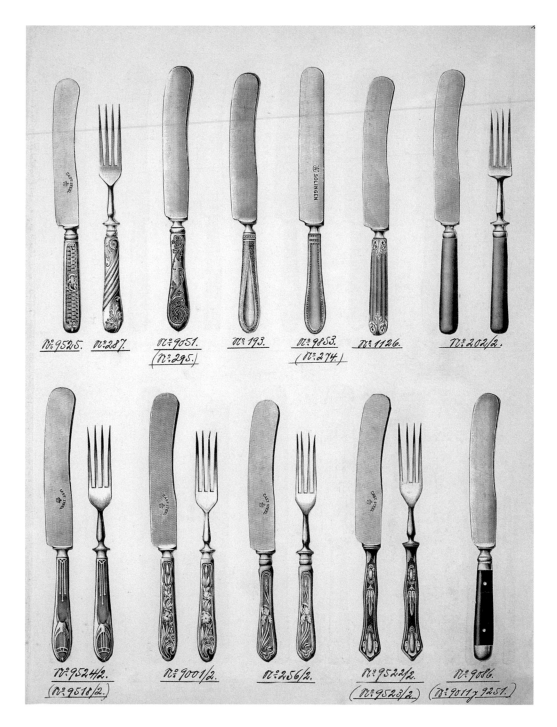

Nᵒ 9525.   Nᵒ 287.   Nᵒ 9051.   Nᵒ 193.   Nᵒ 9853.   Nᵒ 1126.   Nᵒ 202/2.

(Nᵒ 295.)   (Nᵒ 274.)

Nᵒ 9524/2.   Nᵒ 9001/2.   Nᵒ 256/2.   Nᵒ 9522/2.   Nᵒ 9086.

(Nᵒ 9518/2.)   (Nᵒ 9523/2.) (Nᵒ 9011 y 9251.)

This chaotic advertisement for a Lancashire brewery's finest uses a design of golden barley and cheerful blue cornflowers against a summer sky to emphasize the ales' health giving properties. Customers at public houses are advised here to insist on seeing the label to be sure that the beer poured into their glasses does indeed come out of the bottles ordered.

explored fully in the twentieth century, was difficult for the average home-maker to absorb. Many people of this exciting, pivotal mid-century age, however, shared at least Eastlake's tendency both to look back to the certainties of the past and forward to a new and untested industrial style. Urbanites and suburbanites were attached both to frivolous and sentimentalized representations, be it dairy cows or sculpted acorns, of the rural life they had now escaped, and to the innovative decorative possibilities opened up by newly invented, chemically produced colours. Mauve and magenta had only just been synthesized and were understandably all the rage, offering a brightness that Nature could not emulate, and considerations of which were beside the fashion point.

The Veneerings of Dickens' *Our Mutual Friend* were unlikely to receive Eastlake's accolades either, remaining resolutely immune to instruction. 'There was a time when it was thought tasteful to let every knick-knack for the table assume an appearance which utterly belied its real purpose,' says Eastlake. 'Some of my readers may remember the little gilt Cupid wheeling a barrow of salt, which once appeared in many an English dining-room.' At a dinner party *chez* the Veneerings, Dickens notes that on the table 'a caravan of camels take charge of the fruits and flowers and candles, and kneel down to be loaded with the salt'.

Some other improving manuals of home decoration took a less austere tone. Rhoda and Agnes Garrett, for example, giving their *Suggestions for House Decoration* in 1876, provide down-to-earth descriptions of the decorative problems of houses as they are now and provide alternatives for better arrangements in houses as they might be. They suggest a change from 'the dingy and dreary solemnity of the modern London dining-room' to one that could instead be treated to plainer wallpapers, and where anything 'over floral' could be avoided and intimidating portrait paintings removed.

58 (The Garretts, though, still complain about the introduction of mauve and magenta to the decorative palette.) Their advice, as here for the choice of dining table, is precise and practical:

> In a small room a table about seven feet long and three feet six inches wide will be found much more sightly and convenient than a telescope table of the usual enormous width, which fills up the space and hardly leaves room for the servant to pass without rubbing the paint off the wall on one side, and setting fire to her skirts on the other.

The Garretts call for simple and comfortable dining chairs; sideboards that are practical, not mock-medieval styles with 'hideous caricatures of every animal and vegetable form'; a well-designed chandelier; and a Turkey carpet and a border either of parquet or dark-coloured drugget.

Writing in 1901, Violet Biddle gives sound advice about 'graceful and airy' flowers for table decoration, ones that are flat and do not obstruct the view across the table as early Victorian creations were wont to do. 'Simplicity is the great cry now,' she says. She considers blue flowers unsuitable for dinner tables as they turn brown or dull mauve in artificial light, but points out that bright red or yellow glows well in gaslight. In

The parvenu Veneering family and guests are seated at their 'bran-new' dinner table in an illustration to Charles Dickens' Our Mutual Friend of 1864–5. Illustrator Marcus Stone has captured the clutter of a pretentiously over-crowded table, awash with glasses and with an over-the-top, zoomorphic central épergne, crowned with an expensive pineapple. The diners exude an air of anxiety rather than relaxation.

First Prize for Table Decoration, Royal Horticultural Society, 1851.

This engraving is of the first-prize-winning table decoration at the Royal Horticultural Society in 1851. The design uses three épergnes, with fruit, flowers and foliage around the bases and in single bowls at the top of the stems. The tallest would be placed at the centre of a long table, each of the smaller ones towards an end. The centrepiece arrangement appears to be a novel one of raspberries on the vine.

1860, our friend 'Tabitha Tickletooth' (who, incidentally, is depicted as the frontispiece of her book, a stout and fierce housewife, looking suspiciously like a portrayal of the real – male – author of *The Dinner Question*, actor Charles Selby, in drag) also suggests that large candelabra will block the views of guests. She recommends instead contemporary plaited wick lamps that are safe and give a bright light. She warns against too many flames, which give out too much heat. Mrs Orrinsmith, writing about art for the home in 1876, considers gas lighting too hard for a dinner party, and suggests that 'No light is so charming as that of many candles, be it for general effect or for particular purposes…'. For the important art of napkin-folding, the nineteenth-century housewife could refer to editions of Mrs Beeton and other manuals for a variety of suitable designs. The suggested edifices were of a complexity that would keep at least one servant busy for

60 an entire afternoon – fans and water lilies and mitres were sculpted like origami from starched white damask.

The consistent advice that rings out from all these volumes is that interior styles should be simplified and that the High Victorian clutter of the 1850s should be abandoned for good. And no detail should be ignored. As one mid-century advice manual put it: 'It is hardly possible to attach too much importance to the minor arts of pleasing practised in all highly civilized society.' The next couple of decades saw a confusion of different solutions to the problem – some in imitation of classical styles, some neo-Georgian, others a more bohemian, pared-back Aesthetic style. But these ideas were explored by an informed minority rather than the majority, who may have taken some heed but otherwise happily kept their rooms awash with the ornament that they enjoyed. It was not until the turn of the nineteenth and twentieth centuries that simpler styles and lighter, airy rooms became really established.

The niceties of dining

The house, the table, the food and the guests at a Victorian dinner party were all dressed up for

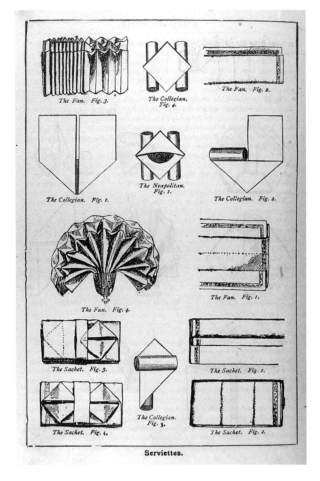

Napkin, or serviette, folding was an essential art form in a middle-class Victorian household. The task would not have been made any easier by trying to follow the instructions on these two pages from an edition of Mrs Beeton's Every-day Cookery. The stages here for seven designs – The Fan, The Collegian, The Neapolitan

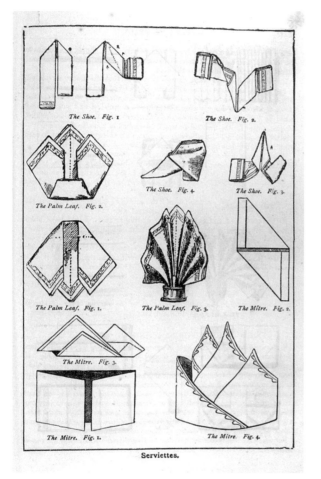

The Shoe. Fig. 1   The Shoe. Fig. 2.

The Shoe. Fig. 4.   The Shoe. Fig. 3.

The Palm Leaf. Fig. 2.

The Palm Leaf. Fig. 1.   The Palm Leaf. Fig. 3.   The Mitre. Fig. 2.

The Mitre. Fig. 3.

The Mitre. Fig. 1.   The Mitre. Fig. 4.

Serviettes.

and The Sachet, The Shoe, The Palm Leaf and The Mitre – are illustrated out of their correct order (although they are numbered).

the occasion. And so, too, were the servants. One way in which to demonstrate material success was in the conspicuous display of a number of flunkies to wait on your guests. The trick might well be to make it look as though these servants were your regular attendants, but often they were hired for the evening, and some were less well qualified for the job than others. At a banquet given by Dickens' Veneerings, 'Four pigeon-breasted retainers in plain clothes stand in line in the hall' and Thackeray, in his *The Book of Snobs*, asks whether you

> …get in cheap made dishes from the pastry-cook's, and hire a couple of green-grocers, or carpet-beaters, to figure as footmen, dismissing honest MOLLY, who waits on common days, and bedizening your table (ordinarily ornamented with willow-pattern crockery) with twopenny-halfpenny Birmingham plate. Suppose you pretend to be richer and grander than you ought to be—you are a Dinner-giving Snob.

Thackeray is particularly scathing about those who spare no expense on ostentation but scrimp on the food and drink, such as '…my friend LADY MACSCREW, who has three grenadier flunkies in lace round the table, and serves up a scrag of mutton on silver, and dribbles you out bad sherry

62 and port by the thimblefuls…'. He chastises that guests should be brought together in a natural way to enjoy ordinary, unpretentious, everyday family meals, not overblown dinners, which are an unnecessary source of anxiety, even misery:

> The hostess is smiling resolutely through all the courses, smiling through her agony; though her heart is in the kitchen, and she is speculating with terror lest there be any disaster there. If the *soufflé* should collapse, or if WIGGINS does not send the ices in time—she feels as if she would commit suicide—that smiling, jolly woman!

Tabitha Tickletooth is of the same opinion, suggesting in her hints for dinner parties that hosts should concentrate on a few good dishes rather than 'kickshaws' and side-dishes, and that they should not try to 'astonish the Browns'. A perfect dinner can be just a good soup, a small turbot, a neck of venison and an apricot tart.

Such words fell on a considerable number of deaf ears, with dinners prepared at home consisting of as many as twenty or thirty choices of dish, elaborately decorated and served. 'It is in serving up food that is at once appetizing and wholesome that the skill of the modern housewife is severely tasked,' says Mrs Beeton. 'Hams and tongues should be ornamented with cut vegetable flowers, raised pies with aspic jelly cut in dice,' she advises. Her generally sensible approach still suggests menus of an elaboration that we would not countenance today at even the grandest of restaurants. Although guests were not expected to partake of every item on the menu, they were still likely to come away with a stomach churning a bilious mix of fish and meats and sugar. One Beeton menu, for example, has *all* of the following included in its suggested dishes: turbot, cod, eels, sole, pike, chicken, mutton, lobster, oysters, partridges, sweetbreads, beef, turkey, ham, grouse, pheasants and hare. Luckily, they are accompanied by

Another character from Thackeray's The Book of Snobs puffs himself up to illustrate a chapter lobbying for straightforward entertaining. 'Your usual style of meal—that is, plenteous, comfortable, and in its perfection—should be that to which you welcome your friends, as it is that of which you partake yourself.'

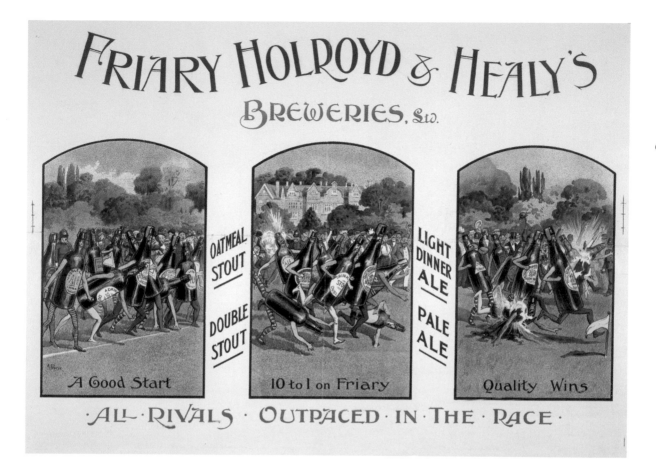

This beer advertisement with its curious race of bottles dressed like medieval knights looks as though it could owe some creative inspiration to Lewis Carroll, whose Alice's Adventures in Wonderland was published in 1865.

salad, artichokes and stewed celery, although a manual of the 1880s states: 'Salad, which occupies a very subordinate place at English dinner-tables, is much appreciated in France…'. Then the diners move on to desserts of Italian cream, apple Charlotte, pear compote, pastry, punch jelly and iced pudding. It is no wonder that middle-class Victorians were obsessed with their poor digestions, and that many advertisements for dealing with the problem appeared alongside those for processed and packaged foods in contemporary magazines and on shop fronts. There was Eno's Fruit Salt, for example, which carried the exhortation: 'Don't suffer from injudicious eating or congestion from lack of exercise.' A medicine called Antipon dealt with another result of dining habits: 'The Great Permanent Cure for

64   Corpulence'. Writing in 1929 and commenting on twentieth-century changes in eating habits due to problems of health, Frances, Countess of Warwick recalls that:

> Health Reform movements … have substituted food faddists for gourmets at our dinner-tables. As a great many of the gourmets of thirty years ago and earlier used to suffer shockingly, and often died before they were sixty, the change is to the good. But some glamour goes with it, and a few may sigh when they remember the houses where you were "done well".

The choice of guests around the table who were to be 'done well' was critical. 'Avoid "bores" of every kind,' directs Tabitha Tickletooth, 'the parliamentary, the literary, and scientific varieties above all; and do not, as many eccentric persons often do, congregate oddities together.' A.V. Kirwan, writing in 1864 in *Host and Guest: a book about dinners,* in haughty tones advises a mix of guests to promote good conversation:

> But your good talker should be an urbane and polite man, not bumptious and underbred. Barristers and travelled physicians are generally excellent company, though the former not seldom monopolise too much of the conversation, and give it occasionally a shoppy air.

Kirwan's advice might have seemed rather alarming to the *nouveaux riches,* as he goes on to maintain that a good guest should be a 'born gentleman' as 'early training' in matters of etiquette and conversation are indispensable; those without it are 'social pests'. In the 1880s in a magazine article about etiquette, the values of conversation at dinner were nicely pointed out: 'Any approach to lengthy descriptions of purely personal adventure cannot fail to be out of place at a dinner-table, where the obvious business of the company is to consume, and not to listen.'

*Two examples of food and recipe illustrations from editions of Mrs Beeton demonstrate an unfussy style for presentation of even the simplest dishes. The appearance of the vegetables and salad (**above**) and the fish and sea food (**right**) might then be emulated by a middle-class cook.*

Oysters.

Dressed Crab.

Whitebait.

Lobster

Brochet of Smelts.

Red Mullet in cases.

Salmon

Brill

Turbot

Whiting.

Eels

Mackerel

Haddock

Cod

Trout.

Soles.

Guests abided by complicated rules of etiquette that could dictate every movement from the manner of walking into a dining room through to the way in which different items of food should be consumed. Needless to say, guidance was on offer in these matters, too, often from members of the upper classes who were perceived to be *au fait* with desired ways of doing things. A 'Member of the Aristocracy' achieved publishing success with *Manners and Rules of Good Society or Solecisms to be Avoided*, which was in its twenty-sixth edition by 1902. This book of new etiquette considers dinner giving the 'most important of all social observances' and a 'means of enlarging a limited acquaintance'. In fact, 'a reputation for giving good dinners is in itself a passport to fashionable society.' No detail is left to chance, with particular attention given to the manner in which different foods should be eaten and with which implements. Soup should always be eaten with a tablespoon, the Aristocrat reminds his or her readers, and a dessert spoon should be for other

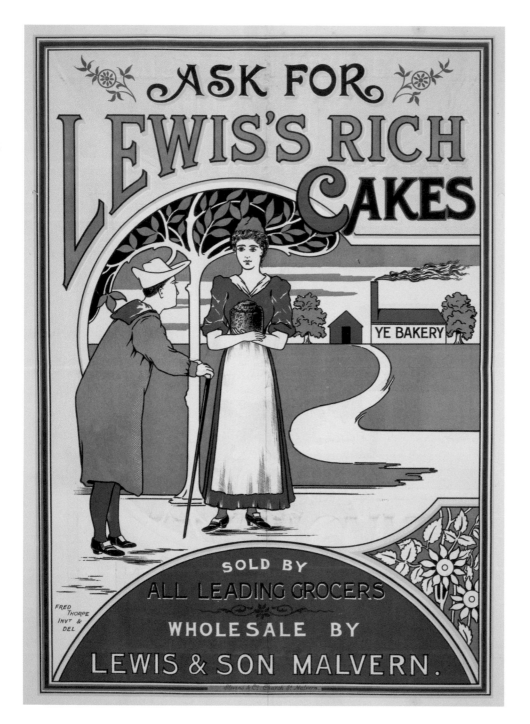

The attractive graphic design of this advert appears to have an interesting mix of influences. Although its premise is wholesomely old worldly, suggesting cakes fashioned at 'Ye Bakery', the tree and the path are of a sinuous, stylized Art Nouveau character. A Continental feel is furthered by the dress of the two figures, which does not look as though it would ever have been seen in Malvern, England.

purposes, 'such as for eating fruit tarts, custard-puddings … All made dishes, such as *quenelles*, *rissoles*, patties, ec., should be eaten with a fork only… In eating asparagus, a knife and fork should be used, and the points should be cut off and eaten with a fork as is sea-kale, ec.' In removing the stones of fruit from the mouth, '…either the dessert-spoon or fork should be raised to the lips to receive the stones, which should be placed at the side of the plate…'. Peas, it is stated firmly and as we all remember, should be eaten with a fork. There is clear advice for the behaviour of women gourmets: 'As a matter of course young ladies do not eat cheese at dinner parties.' Whether this was because a young lady's constitution was deemed insufficiently strong to tolerate powerful cheese flavours or whether it was thought undignified for her to breathe cheesy exhalations is unclear. Some of the detail even has a grotesque edge – most unappetizing.

> As regards small pigeons, golden plovers, snipe, quails, larks, etc., a whole bird is given to each help, and the proper way to eat these birds is to cut the meat from the breast and wings and to eat each morsel at the moment of cutting it; the bird should not be turned over and over on the plate, or cut in half or otherwise dissected.

Should you have been tempted to pick up any of these morsels it might have been difficult to restore yourself to elegance. Tabitha Tickletooth says that finger bowls are to be banned, as they have been 'disgustingly abused'; instead, the corner of a napkin could be dipped into rose water and dabbed to the mouth or hands.

Modern styles at table

In the second half of the nineteenth century in Britain, it was *de rigueur* to present smart dishes and menus in French. The pre-eminence of French

68 cooking, demonstrated by emigré chefs such as Alexis Soyer and later Auguste Escoffier, established at the Savoy Hotel by 1890, was widely acknowledged in fashionable society. Even Mrs Beeton, the sensible English cook, allows French to creep into the titles of her dishes, sometimes in hybrid form. Her dinner party menus contain dishes such as 'Peas à la Française', 'Boiled Mackerel à la Mâitre d'Hôtel' and 'Charlotte à la Vanille'. The use of the French 'à la' indicates the way in which the dish has been prepared, becoming a sort of shorthand that would need to be decoded by the cook or the diner, for whom the meaning was not always clear. Some advice manuals of the time suggested that a tendency to cook French recipes should be avoided; that it was not English menus that were

This suggested table setting from around 1890 illustrates dining in the by then old-fashioned 'à la Française' style, in which dishes are placed on the table and passed around by servants, hosts and guests. The elaborate, arching floral decoration, which blocks sight-lines between guests, is also looking dated.

This 1876 image from an edition of Punch *shows the fashionable new style of dining 'à la Russe': servants deliver dishes from a sideboard while the table is left unencumbered. A long centrepiece arrangement of flowers and fruits takes up a large area of the table space, and is in a modern, low-level style.*

the problem, but rather the shortcomings of English cooks.

Late Victorian dinners given at home were now almost without exception organized in a style described, predictably, in French as *à la Russe*. Although the term was widely used, the actual nature of the style required was open to some interpretation. A.V. Kirwan is predictably unconvinced about the ability of the middle class to understand the term properly:

> Of late years people who give dinners give them what is called *à la Russe*; but if you ask nine out of every ten what they mean by dining *à la Russe*, they are unable to tell you. All they can say is, that there is nothing on the table but flowers and fruits, that the dishes are carved on the sideboard and handed about to the guests.

In fact, this is a fair description. Previously, dishes would be delivered to the table in tureens and passed around by the guests or by servants, with the host carving joints of meat at the table, in an arrangement called *à la*

Française. The simpler *à la Russe* method of their supply from the sideboard or a side-table meant that the dining table was less congested with tableware or overloaded with an exhausting array of choices. The table was left to cutlery, wine glasses, beautifully folded damask napkins (perhaps containing a bread roll for each guest), arrangements of flowers, candelabra and bowls of fruit. Calls were for a style that was clean and fresh. The much-loved Victorian *épergne*, an ornament, usually silver, for the centre of a dinner table, might even be abandoned. An *épergne* is a stand, often of more than one tier or with branches, to hold fruit or flowers. It was precisely the sort of object that could clutter up a table and obscure the guests' view of each other, and could perhaps be replaced with smaller, less

This is a very grand late Victorian dinner. The dining room is capacious and the guests are dressed up to the nines. Magnificent silver candelabra dominate the table, which is laid with course upon course worth of cutlery and wine glasses, and with damask napkins folded in two different designs. The candlelight reflecting off this impressive volume of silver and glass would be dazzling.

tall arrangements of flowers and simpler bowls of fruit. Each guest's place setting was to have three glasses, for sherry or Madeira, claret and hock, and it was suggested that the hock glass be coloured. Coloured glasswares were fashionable, and helped the guests to distinguish one drinking vessel from another. But even in such apparently simple matters as the choice of wine glass, advice was confusing. Coloured glass was pretty and useful, but was to be treated with caution. 'Carried to excess,' warns an advice manual of the 1880s, 'the contrast of showy colours is rather vulgar-looking than not, and is more suggestive of a railway refreshment-room than the quiet taste that should regulate such matters in a private house.' Champagne, if served, was drunk from a sparkling broad and shallow *tazza*, which fashionably replaced the old tall and narrow flutes.

At the end of the meal *à la Russe*, delicious and decorative desserts, jellies and ices were placed on the table in display, rather than being served from the side. Kirwan notes that dessert is an Italian invention, and hopes that it might be kept simple as 'it is often a dangerous superfluity, and the fruitful cause of many an indigestion'. Ices are less heavy on the stomach and very fashionable: 'The ices most in vogue in London are pine, lemon, orange, ginger, strawberry, and cherry ices. In Paris, apricot, peach, chocolate, coffee, and four fruit ices are more common than with us.' If served,

The calm and unflustered demeanour of this young cook must have reflected the relief of many spared the time and effort of preparing towering jellies from basic ingredients by the advent of prepared, packaged alternatives. One jelly here contains fruit salad, another is the 'Cocoa & Chocolate' of the pack on the left; and sundae glasses contain mixed pieces of chopped fruit jelly.

72 such mouth-watering ices might well be delivered direct to the door during a dinner party. Their preparation was complicated, requiring block ice that would be unavailable to most households, and there was danger of their melting due to basic or non-existent refrigeration at home. While conceding that 'at some evening parties, ices are scarcely to be dispensed with', Mrs Beeton nevertheless cautions that they can be dangerous. The aged, delicate and children should abstain (it is unlikely that children would agree), and even the strong and healthy should eat them only in moderation, and at an interval after the meal suitable to digestion being already under way. They should not be eaten at all if the person is very warm or after violent exercise 'as in some cases they have produced illnesses which have ended fatally'. Beeton suggests that desserts should be garnished with leaves; that fruit bowls are enhanced with grapes hanging from the border of the dish 'in a *négligé* sort of manner'; and that candied fruits and confections, including chocolate, are now indispensable.

Drinking at home

Such rich and substantial dinners were washed down with a mix of alcohol that would alarm us

MODERN MODE OF SERVING DISHES.

S 1. Jelly of two colours.   T 1. Raspberry Cream.   U 1. Centre Dish of Various Fruits.
V 1. Trifle.   W 1. Strawberries au naturel in ornamental Flowerpot.

A demonstration of Mrs Beeton's 'modern mode' of serving desserts includes a two-tier jelly, a raspberry cream and a decorated trifle. 'At fashionable tables,' she remarks, 'forced fruit is served growing in pots, these pots being hidden in more ornamental ones, and arranged with the other dishes.'

Marbled Jelly

Blanc-Mange

Trifle

Almond Puddings.

Rout Cakes.

Jam Pudding

Tartlets.

Mince Pies

Vanilla Cream.

Apple Marmalade Tart

Cherry Tart

Pear & Apple Dumplings

Dessert Biscuits.

Charlotte Russe.

Gingerbread Pudding

Fruit Tart.

Milk Pudding

Christmas Plum Pudding.

Apples & Rice.

Pancakes

'A dessert would not now be considered complete without candied and preserved fruits and confections. The candied fruits may be purchased at a less cost than they can be manufactured at home. They are preserved abroad in most ornamental and elegant forms.' Thus advised Mrs Beeton in 1861

today and which, indeed, alarmed a number of observers at the time. Our Aristocrat in *Manners and Rules of Good Society* describes the procession of drink at a fashionable dinner:

> Sherry is always drunk after soup, hock either with oysters before the soup or with fish after the soup, and Chablis sometimes takes the place of hock. Champagne is drunk immediately after the first *entrée* has been served, and so during the remainder of dinner until dessert. Claret, sherry, port, and Madeira are the wines drunk at dessert, and not champagne, as it is essentially a dinner wine.

Unsurprisingly he also tells us that 'Ladies are not supposed to require a second glass of wine at dessert, and passing the decanters is principally for the gentlemen.'

A.V. Kirwan gives detailed information about drinks in polite society, providing a striking picture of what was consumed in fashionable circles in the 1860s. He catalogues liqueurs, ales and beer, perry and champagnes and wines. He notes that during the previous sixteen years (to 1864) consumption of champagne doubled in England. In 1831, 254,000 gallons of French wine were imported, but by 1861 that figure had risen to 2,227,000 gallons. The extra couple of million gallons here is an interesting reflection on the

74

The quantities of fine wines, such as the German Moselle advertised here, imported into Britain grew substantially in the second half of the nineteenth century. This increase was a response to the growing numbers of people who could afford to buy wines, and to the styles of dining that required them to be served.

development of social habits – and of disposable income, conspicuous consumption and leisure time – as the English settled into an industrial age. In the 1860s and 1870s even an average family spent about fifteen per cent of the weekly expenditure on drink. It comes as no surprise, then, that 'gout rests' to prop up swollen and throbbing toes were part of the furniture of gentlemen's clubs.

Kirwan says that it is 'impossible to deny that wine, taken in moderation, tends to strengthen and excite the spirits, to cheer and comfort the languid, and to refresh the toil-worn and exhausted.' He considers Graves an excellent table wine and a good substitute for Chablis; that there is nothing better than a good vintage Beaune; and that Macon travels well. He talks about champagne, claret, German wines, Malaga and other Spanish wines, and comments on the use of French grape varieties in New South Wales and in the Cape. He considers that too great a variety of wines at the dinner table is not commended, and does not miss his opportunity to have a dig at those who are not wine *cognoscenti*: '...to reserve Burgundy for the *entremets*, *sucrés*, or dessert, is a piece of rampant snobbishness worthy of a *nouveau riche*.'

The evidence that Kirwan is a dreadful snob oozes constantly from the pages of his book. 'Schubagh' is, he says, a 'horrid burning beverage' invented in Ireland. He describes it as a decoction of barley, tinged with an infusion of saffron, sweetened with sugar, to which is added spirits of wine to give it strength. Beer is not usually drunk with dinner and if it is, he says dismissively, it would most likely only happen in some parts of London. Cider is only drunk with meals in the country and in the provinces. And the drinking habits of women are itemized in disparaging terms: 'At the mid-day meal called lunch, also, beer is an article not unfrequently [*sic*] taken by those young ladies who exhibit so little appetite for dinner at fashionable

76 tables at eight o'clock.' It would not be unusual, in fact, for the middle or upper classes to drink alcohol at every meal of the day, including breakfast. The Aristocratic adviser, for example, describes a grand breakfast, to be served at ten or eleven o'clock: 'the meal somewhat resembles luncheon, fish, entrées, game and cold viands being given, with the addition of tea, coffee, and liqueurs'.

'The best way for any gentleman desiring to stock a cellar, is to go to a first-rate wine merchant of position and character,' says Kirwan, and this is no doubt precisely what Charles Dickens did. The contents of Dickens' wine cellar at his house in Gad's Hill were sold after his death at an auction in August 1870, and give some insight into the drinking tastes of a professional man of distinction. The cellars contained cider, sherries, Madeira, port, many fine wines, champagnes, Sauternes, hocks, milk punch, kirsch, Curaçao, cordial gin, pineapple rum, brandies and whisky. From such supplies as these, many delicious and highly alcoholic concoctions could be prepared. In *Cups and their Customs*, written by Henry Porter and George E. Roberts in 1863, there are recipes for hot wine cups and cold cups, juleps and punches and hot ale cups. The authors give basic recipe advice for their preparation, such as that hot cups should never be boiled as the spirit evaporates; that cold cups need ice; and that when using lemon peel the pith should be discarded as its taste is poor. The most important herb for flavouring drinks is borage, plus mint for juleps, or verbena, and they say that a thin slice of cucumber peel can be used as a substitute. (Borage has a flavour similar to cucumber, and is rarely used today, perhaps because cucumbers are now so easily acquired.)

The Toad Rock is a famous sandstone formation at Rusthall Common, outside Tunbridge Wells, which bears a striking resemblance to the amphibian. This advertisement for a local brewery adds cartoon parts of the toad, who is enjoying a bottle of its light bitter ale.

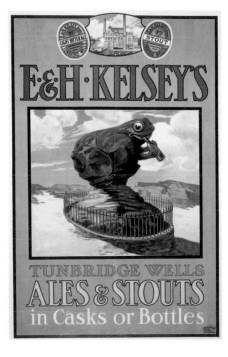

A guest at a country house is invited to view the cellars by an affable butler in a Punch cartoon of 1876. 'Ah! Ha!' he exclaims on encountering a substantial supply of whisky: 'So you've been laying in the fashionable drink, I see! The doctors are all mad about it.' It was taken for granted at the time by many, including members of the medical profession, that alcohol helped restore good health.

Porter and Roberts recommend that a good punch can be made with sugar, hot water, lemons, old Jamaica rum, brandy, porter or stout and a dash of arrack (an Eastern spirit fermented from the coco-palm or from rice and sugar). A julep is made of ice with white sugar, brandy, rum and the outer rind of lemon. It is shaken to mix, decorated with a sprig of mint and drunk 'via a straw or a stick of macaroni'. Dickens' milk punch would most likely have been made with the rind of lemons and Seville oranges, pale brandy, rum and grated nutmeg, to which the lemon and orange juice are then added together with water and boiling milk. It is then filtered and bottled. Wine cups are made with claret or burgundy and the addition of sherry, or curaçao (a bitter orange liqueur), noyau (a brandy liqueur flavoured with fruit kernels) or pineapple syrup, well iced, garnished with lemon peel and with added soda water and sprigs of borage. For a hot ale cup the ale is heated, gin and sherry are added, along with American bitters and cloves, cinnamon and sugar. Cheers!

78 *Backlash*

When describing a visit to 'Country Snobs' in his book of 1852, Thackeray has his narrator deplore both their drinking and eating habits. He is served Marsala, but would have preferred sherry; port is offered and 'Hollands and water', which, when it arrives, he finds is actually gin and hot water. The country dinner depends on the animal just killed for the purpose, so that 'the pig being consumed, we began upon a sheep'. Game is served up with ridiculous 'great state', but in fact 'consisted of a landrail, not much bigger than a corpulent sparrow'. Highly entertaining, it nevertheless all sounds excessive and disgusting and is intended to do so. Thackeray is satirizing the extents of drinking, slaughter and eating that his country characters are prepared to go to in their futile attempts to impress their narrator guest with their grandiose hospitality. From the first half of the nineteenth century and increasingly over its decades, there was also a growing concern about the effects on health of such overindulgence, and about the moral degeneration of which it appeared to be a symptom. There came impassioned cries for a reappraisal of eating and drinking habits.

Excessive consumption of meat and drink was, however, a problem of affluence, or at least a good basic wage, and was not one that affected the poor. Many people, both in towns and in rural locations, were lucky to eat any meat at all and were more likely to drink brews of tea than of beer. At best, the meat they did manage to get might be a fatty strip of bacon once a week to supplement a diet based almost exclusively on bread, with a scraping of margarine, potatoes and an occasional treat of a dumpling. In the 1840s as many as two million people in Britain lived on potatoes alone, and in

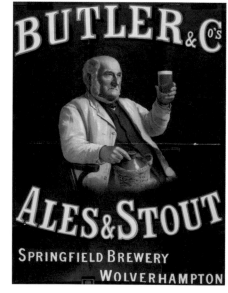

A kindly gent pours his glass of beer from a stone flagon encased in protective wickerwork. The man has a sober, serious and comfortable appearance, and was the brewery's trademark.

CHAPTER XXVII.

A VISIT TO SOME COUNTRY SNOBS.

WE had the fish, which, as the kind reader may remember, I had brought down in a delicate attention to Mrs. Ponto, to variegate the repast of next day; and cod and oyster-sauce, twice laid, salt cod and scolloped oysters, formed parts of the bill of fare until I began to fancy that the Ponto family, like our late revered monarch George II., had a fancy for stale fish. And about this time, the pig being consumed, we began upon a sheep.

Thackeray's narrator pays a visit to some country varieties in his The Book of Snobs. As elsewhere, he finds country snobs set on giving an appearance of being wealthier and more cultivated that they actually are; their particular proclivity is for an excess of dinner dishes based on the particular farm animal killed for the occasion of their entertaining.

Ireland the figure was doubled to four million – about half the population of the entire country.

These people were malnourished, and could be described as reluctant vegetarians, while the middle classes ate the proceeds of the industrial revolution. The backlash against the habits of the latter that led to the establishment of a Vegetarian Society started in the conurbation of Manchester and Salford among Nonconformists in the 1830s. It was strongly linked to romantic and revolutionary-democratic ideas that had, for example, been expressed by an inspirational precursor – the vegetarian poet Percy Bysshe Shelley, often quoted by passionate, like-minded followers later in the nineteenth century. In Book VIII of his poem *Queen Mab* of 1813, written when he was twenty-one, Shelley describes an arcadia in which man, no longer a flesh-eater, lives harmoniously with nature in a 'paradise of peace'. With the purification of man's eating habits comes purification of his temperament and morals – and an escape from one of the currencies of an inequitable society:

...no longer now
He slays the lamb that looks him in the face,
And horribly devours his mangled flesh,
Which, still avenging Nature's broken law,

Within the image (labels):
ALDERMEN FED on early Green Peaz ⊂ THIS WAY~

To the Farinaceous Department.

ON POTATOES ONLY

Young Gentleman Properly Fed upon RADISHES

FED ON CARROTS

CLASS I

REMARKABLE Vegetarian little BOY fed upon TURNIPS TOM-NODDIAN MEDAL

Old Child fed upon Beet Root CLASS IV

Old M'r Gooseberry Fed upon The Fruit of That Name BIARDBAKE MEDAL

CLASS I

SOLD

SOLD

SOLD

80

Kindled all putrid humors in his frame,
All evil passions and all vain belief,
Hatred, despair and loathing in his mind,
The germs of misery, death, disease and crime.
No longer now the wingèd habitants,
That in the woods their sweet lives sing away,
Flee from the form of man; but gather round,
And prune their sunny feathers on the hands
Which little children stretch in friendly sport
Towards these dreadless partners of their play…

Nineteenth-century vegetarians were considered by many to be misguided eccentrics, as this cartoon of a 'Grand Show of Prize Vegetarians', published in Punch in 1852, demonstrates. The premise here is the effect wrought on the body by an over-dependence on one variety of fruit or vegetable.

In *Vindication of Natural Diet* of 1813, Shelley exhorts: 'Never take any substance into the stomach that once had life.' In 1886 Shelley is described as 'a light in the darkness' by H.S. Salt in his publication *A Plea for Vegetarianism*. Salt champions vegetarianism as moral, wholesome and economical, and writes that the practice of flesh-eating is not only cruel towards animals but degrading to men. His moral stance is one that is aware of social, and thus dietary, divisions in the nation: '…we see our upper classes rioting in degrading wastefulness, while our lower classes are sunk in degrading want…'. Salt makes a particular attack on members of the 'aesthetic' and 'artistic' classes who are deeply concerned with matters of taste in their furniture and table decoration, but so little engaged with matters of true taste in their choice of food. The high levels of meat eating that characterize these classes are, he says, incompatible with bright, pure minds. His position was treated with much mirth by many Victorians, and to various parodies; Salt himself was aware that many of his friends regarded a vegetarian 'as little better than a madman'.

The vegetarian movement had other high-profile support, such as that of George Bernard Shaw, who abstained from meat for most of his ninety-four years. His position started from the economical as an impoverished young writer, and he gave up eating meat altogether in 1881 at the age of twenty-five on health and ethical grounds. In fact, Shaw was obsessed with his own health and with his vegetarian diet, which was calculated and prepared with an attention to every last detail of its content and balance successively by his mother, wife and housekeeper. The vegetarianism that started as an economy and developed into an ethical stance became in Shaw something less than wholistically healthy or appealing.

Shaw was also a teetotaller, and Shelley had warned: 'Drink no liquid but water restored to its original purity by distillation.' Henry Salt believed that the purity of the body acquired by eating a fleshless diet led to a greatly reduced craving for alcohol and, incidentally, made smoking tobacco 'almost impossible'. The vegetarian movement was closely linked to the temperance movement, which lobbied to promote abstinence from

82 or moderation in the consumption of alcohol. The movement had its roots in the 1830s in Lancashire, one of the industrial centres where alcohol was perceived to cause many problems of drunkenness and dissolution in its role as a refuge for the urban poor at the coalface of the industrial revolution. Local and national temperance societies followed across the country, increasingly in association with Nonconformist religious groups, such as the Quakers. By the 1870s, after nearly half a century of agitation, the temperance movement attached itself to the Liberal Party in promoting its attempts to use the licensing laws to curtail drinking and drunkenness. Reformers of this period also began to tackle the problem of cleaning up a dirty water supply that was by then known to carry disease – for example, the cholera that rampaged through the cities in the 1830s and 1840s – and had stimulated a public preference for beer over water.

Public houses began to sell non-intoxicating cordials, and the popularity of drinks such as ginger beer, bought both on the street from stalls and in public houses, increased. Although coffee shops were still fashionable, tea, imported in quantity from India from 1830s and cheaper than beer, became the drink of choice (or necessity) for millions, a development on which the temperance movement was quick to capitalize. Not all their initiatives were very successful. 'Temperance Taverns' were established, but their poor quality, non-alcoholic beverages and wearisome proselytizing were no match for the cheery warmth of the public house.

A sombre pair of mid-century illustrations by George Cruikshank (below) contrasts the fortunes of a family that drinks at the gin palace and one that drinks at the water fountain. The former is ragged and argumentative, the latter prosperous and harmonious. 'Aunt Evins on the Temperance "Stump"' (right), at a meeting of the women's temperance association, harangues her audience about the evils of drink, with her evidence seated pathetically on the right.

Although excessive drinking was seen by contemporary social investigators as a problem of the poor, such middle-class disapproval of working-class enjoyments needs to be approached with caution. Drink consistently flowed through almost all Victorian veins, whether it got there via a beer shop or through the wines and liqueurs served at a sumptuous dinner. It was a universal currency, oiling the social wheels in every possible respect. In *Artificial and Compulsory Drinking Usages of the United Kingdom* of 1844, John Dunlop deplores alcohol as a form of reciprocation between the classes. Drink was given as a treat to servants such as washerwomen, whom Dunlop is convinced are set 'on the tipple' by such handouts and are

84 consequently 'killed with kindness'. He himself had seen 'secret assemblies of females' drinking whisky and describes a 'Gypsy Wedding' at which guests were so drunk on whisky that the wedding party descended into a fight. Dunlop also describes middle-class tippling, a particularly shocking aspect of which is 'ladies' forenoon wine-bibbing' and the practice of drinking healths in the morning in brandied wine.

A belief that also straddled the classes was that alcohol was a restorative, strengthening the constitution into the well-built, rosy-cheeked figure that represented then something of a picture of health. Doctors frequently prescribed alcohol as a medicine and, even when the temperance movement began successfully to discredit such ideas, patients put pressure on their medical men to continue to prescribe drink. The further up the social scale the more successful they would have been at a time when doctors were often considered glorified servants rather than specialists to be heeded without question. Dunlop ends his investigation with a testimony from a number of eminent physicians who say that a healthy person is not aided in work or any other way by drink, but that in ill-health alcohol can be used in the same way as other 'stimulant medicines'. It was not until forty or fifty years later, in the 1880s and 1890s and early in the twentieth century, that the parlous state of the nation's health – as a result of poverty and poor diet on the one hand, and overindulgence in food and drink on the other – was realistically addressed. In the meantime, the Victorian parties, whether at glamorous dinners or sparkling public houses, continued.

The whisky drinkers of this 1899 advertisement are depicted as healthy, happy and patriotic, a world away from the images of drunkenness described by the temperance movement. An Irishman and a Scotsman celebrate, while John Bull looks on approvingly.

An ailing lady is offered Barrett's Stout by her doctor and is apparently restored to instant glowing good health by its nourishing properties. The efficacious stout replaces the cup of tea in her sick room, encouraging a widespread Victorian belief that alcoholic drinks were particularly beneficial as medicine.

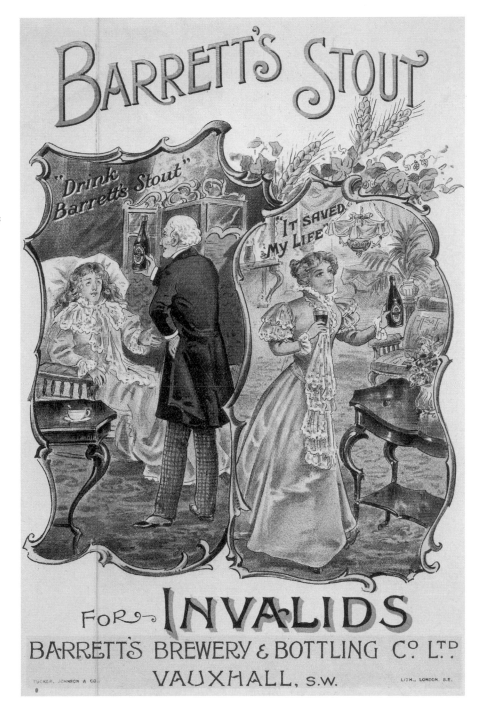

By no means everyone was instructing the cook in the preparation of elaborate dinners for entertaining at home, mixing drinks or sitting down to a substantial plain family dinner. While an air of respectability settled over the sprawling suburbs, a different miasma shrouded the inner cities. Stinking from the manufacturing located at their hearts, urban industrial areas were left largely to the occupation of the labouring poor. In her novel North and South, *first published in 1855, Elizabeth Gaskell's young heroine Margaret Hale moves from the country to 'Milton', a northern textile mill town, after family circumstances change. Gaskell describes their arrival there:*

> For several miles before they reached Milton, they saw a deep lead-coloured cloud hanging over the horizon in the direction in which it lay… Nearer to the town, the air had a faint taste and smell of smoke… Quick they were whirled over long, straight, hopeless streets of regularly-built houses, all small and of brick… People thronged the footpaths … with a slovenly looseness…
>
> 'New Street,' said Mr Hale.

Gaskell's naming of 'New Street', a thoroughfare altogether different in character and appearance from the 'new' enjoyed by Dickens' middle-class Veneerings, with their 'bran-new house in a bran-new quarter of London', would not have been accidental. The 'new' of Milton's urban centre has a lot less polish or promise. A decade later, social investigator Thomas

*A bowler-hatted oyster seller (**right**) pitches his stall, probably in Lancashire, in a photograph of about 1890. Oysters were a staple food until transformed into a luxury by over-fishing. The illustration (**above**) of a top-hatted oyster seller is from an 1864 edition of Henry Mayhew's London Labour and the London Poor.*

Archer describes the state of the housing, an older, decaying stock, in Bethnal Green in London:

> At the end of this blind court there will be found either a number of black and crumbling hovels, forming three sides of a miserable little square, like a foetid tank, with a bottom of mud and slime; or an irregular row of similar tenements, mostly with four small rooms, fronted by rotten wooden palings.

The people who live here, Archer finds, are lucifer-box makers, cane workers, clothes-peg makers, shoemakers and tailors – workers in the service industries to the urban populations of the working city – mostly earning only just enough to keep them from absolute starvation. As he ventures

A London food stall is photographed by John Thomson in 1877 for Street Life in London. *The fare on offer is open to conjecture: perhaps a nice pea-soup for lunch, or hot eels? A makeshift awning provides shelter from the elements for street diners. The solidly constructed stall can be wheeled home at the end of the day.*

towards Spitalfields, Archer finds the homes of weavers, whole families crammed into single rooms. The multi-occupancy houses would not include a stove, even for communal use, and, in any case, lighting a decent fire meant first the purchase of fuel, a significant expense in itself. Archer comments that the weavers' families eat at 'cookshops', cheap establishments that could not be graced with the title of restaurant. He describes the food that was on offer:

> …the cookshop, with its mingled steams and mixed flavours of many
> meats; its great slabs of peasepudding; its long rolls of "spotted" or "plain"
> [suet pudding either with a few currants or without]; its baked potatoes
> and gravy; its ha'poths of "pie-crust"; flat, damp, hot, flabby slabs of greasy
> dough, four inches square; its "faggots" and dense peppery
> saveloys…

No wonder, then, that this hefty, grey, greasy diet would be washed down, or its imprint and other grim recollections clouded, with whatever alcohol many of its sufferers could lay hands on. In *London: A Pilgrimage* of 1872, Blanchard Jerrold describes scenes he witnessed in nearby Whitechapel:

> …demands for gin assailed us on all sides. Women old and
> young, girls and boys in the most woful [*sic*] tatters; rogues of
> all descriptions; brazen-faced lads dancing in the flaring ball-
> rooms on the first floor of the public-houses; even the Fire
> King who was performing before half a dozen sailors, and the
> pot-boy who showed the way up the steep stairs—wanted
> gin—nothing but gin. Some cried for a pint, others for half a
> pint, others for a glass…

The option of the cookshop and a glass of gin was a good one, though, compared to the fate of some other urban poor, such

A down-at-heel lemonade vendor is illustrated by Gustave Doré for Blanchard Jerrold's London: A Pilgrimage *of 1872. His barrel of lemonade has a ring of reusable glasses attached around its girth and a carrying handle so that he can move easily from pitch to pitch and can go and replenish his supplies.*

as that described by A. Mearns in a reformist pamphlet, *The Bitter Cry of Outcast London*, in 1883. Mearns visits many families who have no food to eat at all, or merely a pitiable amount. He describes the single-room home of a consumptive woman with five children and a 'drunken' husband:

> When visited she was eating a few green peas. The children were gone to gather some sticks wherewith a fire might be made to boil four potatoes which were lying on the table, and which would constitute the family dinner for the day.

Not ten miles from the leafy suburbs of Hampstead or Ealing, this other layer of the nineteenth-century class structure unpeeled; but there were still other, less fortunate strata beneath. The cookshop grease was preferable to the food in the workhouse. The unfortunate inmates who had fallen on really hard times could expect a breakfast of gruel or porridge, and if they were old or infirm perhaps tea to drink and a small ration of butter and sugar. Children were given milk with bread at breakfast, which may have been served with dripping or treacle. Dinner might be bread and cheese, or 'pudding' made of suet or rice and perhaps served with gravy or treacle. About once a week the pauper inmates were served meat and potatoes, a luxury probably not available to many outside the workhouse or to the agricultural poor; or soup – a comparatively nourishing brew of onions and other vegetables, with barley or oatmeal as a thickener and a small amount of added meat. Supper was often the same meal as breakfast.

Eating out on the street

In the same year as the Great Exhibition, 1851, Henry Mayhew first published his extraordinary *London Labour and the London Poor*, a groundbreaking piece of social history detailing the lives of ordinary Londoners.

An Italian ice cream seller draws an eager young crowd in a magazine illustration of 1884. The street trade in ices, dominated by Italian traders, was well established by this date.

The work appeared again with additions in 1861. The pioneering breadth of Mayhew's survey has given us a remarkable portrait of the less fashionable side of mid-nineteenth-century London, of the poverty and squalor of the many beneath the veneer of progress and prosperity enjoyed by its more fortunate population. In large part the book is about the teeming life of people on the streets of the capital, so much so that along with the miseries of deprivation and poor health there is a strong sense of a community and of vivacity and humour.

A striking proportion of Mayhew's survey is about the trade in and

An idealized portrait of a street fruit seller (**left**) fixes our gaze in Cherry Ripe by William Frederick Yeames. The young woman's basket is secured at her waist by a shoulder strap, and the tankard is for measuring out the cherries. The 'coster girls' that Mayhew observed in the 1850s lived 'severe' lives, often starting work on the streets at about seven years of age and leaving home to buy produce at market at four or five in the morning.

The ice cream van, 1877 style, (**right, top**) is surrounded by enthusiastic boys in another photograph from Street Life in London. The ice cream seller was quickly becoming established as a favourite, taking trade from the traditional ginger beer seller (**right**), illustrated in mid sales pitch by Gustave Doré in 1872.

consumption of food and drink, from the street sellers of fruit, green stuff, pea soup and hot eels, pickled whelks, fried fish, ham sandwiches, bread, boiled puddings, cakes, tarts, hot-cross and Chelsea buns, ice creams and much else to the water carriers, sellers of milk, ginger beer, lemonade, sherbet, hot elder wine and beer. What emerges is a picture of London's labourers and poor, and of lower middle-class city workers in town from the outer quarters or suburbs, buying and eating their meals out on the street. This was by some necessity for those whose homes were overcrowded and without facilities for cooking or for city workers needing sustenance during a long day. From coffee stalls of the early mornings through to hot pies at night, for most of the day it was possible for Londoners to buy fast food or a takeaway from one of thousands of street stalls. Mayhew describes the scene thus:

> Men and women, and most especially boys, purchase their meals day after day in the streets. The coffee-stall supplies a warm breakfast; shell-fish of many kinds tempt to a luncheon; hot-eels or pea-soup, flanked by a potato 'all hot,' serve for a dinner; and cakes and tarts, or nuts or oranges, with many varieties of pastry, confectionery, and fruit, woo to indulgence in a dessert; while for supper there is a sandwich, a meat pudding, or a 'trotter.'

Mayhew finds the precursors of fish and chips in street sellers with neatly painted wooden trays slung around the neck, papered with clean newspapers with the fried fish and parsley strewn over; a salt-box is 'placed at the discretion of customers'. The trade in baked potatoes, he finds, is only fifteen years old; the sellers bake the potatoes at the bakehouse, then

wheel them out and keep them hot in shining metal potato-cans (later in the century the potatoes were baked in portable ovens on the street). The itinerant trade in pies, says Mayhew, is the most ancient of the street callings of London, and at the time of his writing is under threat from the new and successful trade from pie shops. The meat pies are made of beef or mutton, fish pies of eels and fruit pies of apples, currants, gooseberries, plums, damsons, cherries, raspberries or rhubarb according to the season.

An engraving of 1887 details the baking of hot potatoes in portable ovens wheeled out on the street. The cooked potatoes are kept hot in a compartment above the oven. The boy warming his hands illustrates other attractions of the trade.

The pie man's fate is taken up by another of the period's social commentators, Charles Manby, writing in 1853, who describes the competing pie shops, which are not providing a particularly cosy alternative to the street:

> But though the window might be plate-glass, behind which piles of the finest fruit, joints, and quarters of the best meat, a large dish of silver eels, and a portly china bowl charged with a liberal heap of minced-meat, with here and there a few pies, lie temptingly arranged upon napkins of snowy whiteness, yet there is not a chair, stool, or seat of any kind to be found within. No dallying is looked for, nor would it probably be allowed. 'Pay for your pie, and go,' seems the order of the day.

If the pie man wins the toss, he gets a penny for no pie; if he loses, he gives a pie for nothing. A pie man tells Mayhew that gentlemen out late drinking 'toss when they don't want the pies, and when they win they will amuse themselves by throwing the pies at one another, or at me.'

Then there are the confectioneries – cakes, tarts, biscuits, buns and 'sweeties'. Mayhew finds three-cornered puffs with jam inside, raspberry biscuits, gingerbread, muffins and crumpets. Sweets include almond 'toffy', halfpenny lollipops, bulls' eyes and brandy balls. Sticks of rock are made from loaf sugar and rose acid, and he learns that the 'flavouring—or "scent" as I heard it called in the trade—now most in demand is peppermint'. At this point, the sale of ice cream in the street was a rarity, and Mayhew makes a faulty prediction about its future, in spite of being tipped off by a 'quick-witted street-seller'.

> '…Ices in the streets! Aye, and there'll be jellies next … You'll keep your eyes open, sir, at the Great Exhibition; and you'll see a move or two in the streets, take my word for it…'.

> Notwithstanding the sanguine anticipation of my street friend, the sale of ices in the streets has not been such as to offer any great encouragement to a perseverance in the traffic.

LONDON LABOUR AND THE LONDON POOR. 81

TRUMAN HANBURY & BUXTONS

THE COSTER BOY AND GIRL TOSSING THE PIEMAN
[From a Photograph.]
No. 6. [1864.] G

96 In fact, within a couple of decades the sale of ices in the streets was well established, to the extent that other street traders, particularly ginger beer sellers, were suffering the consequences, finding that they had to ice down their drinks to try to compete with the new enthusiasm. Blanchard Jerrold describes the ice cream vendor in his *Pilgrimage* of 1872:

> Whenever we have travelled in crowded places of the working population, we have found the penny ice-man doing a brisk trade—even when his little customers were blue with the cold. The popular ice-vendor is the fashionable rival of the ginger-beer hawker—an old, familiar London figure.

Ginger beer had become very popular by the 1840s, when there were around two hundred 'fountains' on the streets, and other traders were selling pre-prepared stocks of ginger beer. According to Mayhew, in 1842 there were 1,200 street traders in the drink in London. The traders themselves had origins similar to many others on the streets: some had once been mechanics or gentlemen's servants but had fallen on harder times, and then there were those who were simply 'brought up to the streets'. The ginger beer was purported to contain lime juice, but it was actually lemon juice, mixed with sugar and oil of vitriol to bring out the sharpness of the lemon. Air was pumped through the drink as it was drawn, creating an effervescence and frothiness. The stalls were also to be seen on Sundays in places of recreation – Hampstead Heath, Primrose Hill, Kennington Common, Camberwell Green – and a pretty sight they could be, too:

> Erected at the end of a stall is often a painting, papered on a board, in which a gentleman, with the bluest of coats, the whitest of trousers, the yellowest of waistcoats, and the largest of guardchains or eye-glasses, is handing a glass of ginger-beer, frothed up like a pot of stout, and containing, apparently, a pint and a half, to some lady in flowing white robes, or gorgeous in purple or orange.

Mayhew devotes one fascinating section of his book to 'The River Beer-sellers or Purl-men', who represent a trade separate from the street sellers' along the city's 'silent highway'. These traders quench the thirst of the many classes of the Thames' labourers: sailors aboard corn, coal and timber ships, the 'lumpers' who unload the ships, 'stevedores' who stow the craft, riggers, ballast-heavers, watermen and coal-porters. The 'purl' of his title is beer warmed up nearly to boiling and flavoured with gin, sugar and ginger. The purl-men steer their small skiffs between the chaotic river traffic, pulling up alongside the larger vessels and ringing a bell to announce their presence. The trade is so lucrative that a trusted purl-man can, within a few years, save enough to return to dry land and take on a public house. At the lower end of this river drink trade are 'bumboatmen'

who carry flat tin bottles of spirits and climb aboard ships, keeping an account of who has drunk what until the sailors receive their wages and they can return for payment.

Perhaps the most compelling aspect of Mayhew's narrative is its descriptions of the everyday lives and the characters of the street sellers and its snippets of direct oral history. His passages about costermongers, street sellers of fruit and vegetables (and Mayhew includes fish in this category), are particularly detailed as these are the largest class of street traders. He talks of their origins, their entertainments, their dress, their politics, their relationship with the police ('the hatred of a costermonger to a "peeler" is intense'), their marriages and lack of them, their education and their language. He translates common words from costermonger slang, including

A keg of precious whisky is smuggled ashore in a beautiful Irish bay in this entertaining advertisement of 1891. Even the dog looks keen to secure a snifter. The smugglers are all wearing traditional Irish dress, and even the rowing boat is green.

the verb 'cool', meaning 'to look'. When warning of the approach of a police-man, for example, a costermonger calls 'Cool' or 'Cool him' (look at him). The expression derives from the slang's root in using words backwards (look=kool=cool), so that elsewhere 'no' becomes 'on' and 'pot of beer' becomes 'Top o'reeb'.

The diet of the costermongers described by Mayhew is breakfast at a coffee-stall of a small coffee and two thin slices of bread and butter; dinner of '"block ornaments," as they call the small, dark-coloured pieces of meat exposed on the cheap butchers' blocks or counters', which they take to the tap room of a pub to cook and then eat on the street. If they are in a hurry, they might buy a hot pie from a street stall instead, favouring meat or fruit and never eating eel: '"We never eat eel-pies," said one man to me, "because we know they're often made of large, dead eels. *We*, of all people, are not to be had that way. But the haristocrats eats 'em and never knows the differ-ence."' Saveloys with a pint of beer or a gin is another popular dinner. Only on Sunday will the costermonger eat at home, a joint of mutton and good potatoes. The usual beverage is beer, and Mayhew finds that costermon-gers drink hard, having no other way of spending their leisure time. Some, though, have become teetotallers, although the number of such abstainers is tailing off already from that of three or four years earlier.

Although, arguably, none are as rigorous or effective as Mayhew, many other 'social investigators' and journalists were writing at a similar time and in the decades that followed about London's working classes. Their inten-tions were various, from reportage to reform. Some were compassionate and deeply concerned with social inequalities; others were to modern eyes blinkered and disapproving. Yet others were foreigners, who had come to view the underbelly of the English with, often, shock and distaste. Many were clearly influenced by Mayhew.

One such, in 1881, writes about the trade in watercress, today perhaps a surprising staple of the diet of nineteenth-century working-class city-dwellers. This nutritious, iron-rich salad plant could be grown in shallow rivers or artificial ponds on the outskirts of a city, and was brought in great quantities to market. Its strong, spicy flavour was a bonus when other food might be bland or, worse, semi-putrid to the taste. Watercress sellers were often young girls (and they could be frighteningly young, sometimes no more than six or seven) and attracted pens writing, as here, in saccharine terms:

> In fine weather, in spite of the general squalor of the street-retailers, it is
> rather a pretty sight to see them [the girl sellers] flocking out of the great
> watercress market with their verdant basketfuls and armfuls,
> freshening their purchases under the sun-gilt water of the pump,
> splitting them up into bunches, and beautifying the same to the
> best of their ability to tempt purchasers. The fresh green, and
> even the litter of picked-off wilted leaves, pleasantly remind one
> of the country, in the midst of our dusty, dingy drab wilderness of
> brick and mortar; and there is something bird-like in the cress-
> sellers' cry as one after another raises it.

The writer does encounter a watercress seller near the end of her days whose life is not quite so open to romanticizing, but he still somehow makes her destitution sound enchanting:

> Besides her 'cresses,' this old Peggy sold little bunches of worm-
> like radishes, tiniest posies of wall-flowers and stocks which
> some benevolent gardener had enabled her to make up out of his
> refuse, and mittens and patchwork kettle-holders of her own
> manufacture.

This 'old Peggy', a Mrs Griffiths, collapsed with a fatal heart attack one bitterly cold December morning soon afterwards.

This design for a whisky advertisement was never taken up by a distillery, perhaps because the image of a burglar was not one that companies wanted to project. The burglar himself is cloth-capped and threatening, lacking an ideal whisky drinker's sophistication.

OYSTER DAY.—"PLEASE TO REMEMBER THE GROTTO."—(SEE NEXT PAGE.)

'Oyster Day' from an Illustrated London News of 1851 shows street children cajoling passers-by to throw coppers into their empty shells on 25 July, the annual start of the oyster season. The boys on the left are building a grotto, as the article with the illustration describes: '…the grotto is usually built of inverted oyster-shells piled up conically with an opening in the bases, through which, as night approaches, a lighted candle is placed within…'.

A cup of coffee

The street sellers of food and drink catered to all manner of passing trade, of a variety of professions and classes. To some extent there was a democracy of eating and drinking here on the street, perhaps illustrated best at the coffee stalls. Contemporary sketches and cartoons of the ubiquitous stalls (there were about 300 on the London streets in the 1840s) often illustrate both the comparatively well-dressed, lower middle-class men, women and children, and the ragged, all taking strength from the same steaming brews of coffee. Mayhew observes the stalls in the early morning, many operated by women, serving working men, and other stalls in the night, serving 'fast gentlemen' and 'loose girls' in pursuit of their more shadowy professions. In his *Pilgrimage* of 1872, Jerrold observes an 'army of labour' on its way to work in the city at six o'clock in the morning, grateful for the ministrations of the coffee and potato stalls:

> As they trudge on their way, the younger and lighter-hearted whistling
> defiance to the icy wind, the swift carts of fishmongers, butchers, and

102 greengrocers pass them; and they meet the slow-returning wagons of the market-gardeners, with the men asleep upon the empty baskets. The baked-potato man and the keeper of the coffee-stall are their most welcome friends—and their truest; for they sell warmth that sustains them and does not poison.

The coffee was brewed up in large tin cans, sometimes as many as four to a stall, heated with charcoal burners; a few stalls also served tea and cocoa. Mayhew's estimate for the amount of coffee sold on the street in London in the 1850s was 550,000 gallons a year.

Some coffee stalls were quite elaborate, like portable sheds rather than open stalls, and serving breakfast, too – bread and butter, perhaps saveloys and hard-boiled eggs, and ham sandwiches. The latter were from the 1850s an enormously popular staple snack on the street. Mayhew devotes a small section of his book to the men and boys who sell ham sandwiches, dressed in 'white apron, and white sleeves'. The trade in ham sandwiches was particularly brisk at the doors of theatres and Mayhew estimates that about seventy traders made a living in this way. Altogether, he judges that 436,000 ham sandwiches were sold on the London streets each year.

Meanwhile, those city workers with more time, and a little more money, might seek out one of the numerous coffee houses and take a seat. The phenomenon of London coffee shops had begun in the mid-seventeenth century and, by the turn of the seventeenth and eighteenth centuries, coffee drinking had become enormously fashionable. Soon there were thousands of coffee shops, where gossip circulated and social and business contacts could be made. For example, the

Another illustration from Mayhew's London Labour and the London Poor *shows a coffee stall, perhaps early in the morning. 'The best "pitch" in London,' says Mayhew, 'is supposed to be at the corner of Duke-street, Oxford-street. The proprietor of that stall is said to take full 30s. of a morning, in halfpence.'*

This working man's coffee house in Clerkenwell is doing a brisk trade at 1.30 pm lunchtime, serving coffee, hot meals and alcoholic drinks. This is a respectable, well-organized establishment with communal tables, a place of polite conversation and the reading of newspapers.

Jamaica Coffee House in Cornhill was noted for 'the accuracy and fulness [*sic*] of its West Indian intelligence'. There, respectable merchants trading with Madeira and the West Indies acquired valuable business information about the mail-packets on the West India station or about the merchant vessels making voyages there. Many such coffee houses would serve freshly grilled chops and steaks, which might be eaten as a substantial breakfast, in comfortable surroundings.

By the second half of the nineteenth century, many of the coffee houses that remained (perhaps a thousand in London) had become seedy establishments catering to the working and lower ends of the middle classes – to labourers, cab men, clerks and shop workers. They were characteristically dingy, grimy establishments, often in basements, representing the lowest grade of restaurant. The interiors were divided into stalls, or boxes, with wooden partitions screening narrow wood tables with hard seats and little elaboration. Cheap coffee could be an acrid and even poisonous brew, heavily cut with chicory and sometimes adulterated with other substances, such as baked carrots or ground acorns, to eke out the valuable coffee; and it could even be mixed with lethal red oxide of lead to give it a suitably encouraging colour. This dubious beverage was perhaps served up with a slab of bread with a scraping of butter or margarine. Coffee shops also, increasingly, served tea, which, by contemporary reports, could be equally nasty and adulterated. Breakfast served there might be greasy eggs, bacon, mutton chops, pastry, or red herrings and smoked haddock, reportedly served up on filthy crockery.

Charles Dickens visited a coffee house near Bow Street, which he writes about in an article in the magazine *All the Year Round* in 1860. There he observes a sinister character and his meat pudding:

> …a man in a high and long snuff-coloured coat, and shoes, and, to the best of my belief, nothing else but a hat, who took out of his hat a large cold meat pudding; a meat pudding so large that it was a very tight fit, and brought the lining of the hat out with it. This mysterious man was known by his pudding, for on his entering, the man of sleep brought him a pint of hot tea, a small loaf, and a large knife and fork and plate. Left to himself in his box, he stood the pudding on the bare table, and, instead of cutting it, stabbed it, overhand, with the knife, like a mortal enemy; then took the knife out, wiped it on his sleeve, tore the pudding asunder with his fingers, and ate it all up.

There were other places for the ordinary men and women of cities to eat out and find a little bit of warmth from an open fire and companionship. They could take a piece of meat to a public house and pay for it to be cooked there in front of an open fire; and they could buy meat pies, baked potatoes, bread and cheese at the bar to eat with beer. Or they could just drink. Public houses proliferated at a rate that alarmed the temperance societies. In the 1860s in Britain there was one public house licence issued per 180 of the overall population, providing easy access to drink, either

This barrel label from Banks's Wolverhampton brewery dates from 1879 and is a fair illustration of methods of transportation of beer to public houses at the time. The carthorse is seen crossing country, though, rather than trudging the streets.

'Nonal' is a reference to 'non-alcoholic' in this advertisement for temperance ales and stouts. The newspaper seller may well have had to shout loudly to get his message across when most preferred a pint of beer with the usual alcoholic content.

in house or to take away in jugs filled at a counter. By the 1870s there were 107 around 20,000 public houses in London alone, divided into saloon, lounge and private bars to cater to the expectations of differing classes of eaters and drinkers. For all these premises to stay in business it was clear that a great deal of alcohol was being consumed. Elsewhere in the cities, cheap dining houses for the working man's lunch increased in number, serving up menus heavily based on meat and fish.

Meagre home comforts

For the artisan or labourer of moderate means the most substantial and significant meal of the week, both socially and culinarily speaking, was Sunday dinner, served at around half past one in the afternoon. The tradition of this meal, its preparation occupying the whole of Sunday morning, came to endure across the classes throughout the twentieth century – and, for many people, into the twenty-first. The meal was considered a labour of time and of love for the working-class Victorian housewife, and it might involve the family, with children called into employment to shell peas or peel apples. The menu was typically a roast or boiled joint, three different dishes of vegetables, two different puddings, such as apple pie and rice pudding (or a pudding and tart), with bread and cheese, perhaps celery, and plenty of beer. The meal was served in the best style that the household could afford, with a tablecloth and a limited amount of silver plate – perhaps no more than a cruet stand and a couple of tablespoons. The family dressed neatly for the occasion, guests might be invited, and women would retire – not to the drawing room as in a middle-class household, but to the kitchen – to leave the men to their beer and chat. Although not elaborate, the simple, fresh menu of a Sunday dinner was more appetizing than

The Noakes brewery had operated in Bermondsey, London since the end of the seventeenth century. Both breeds of dog illustrated in this poster were accomplished ratters, and may well have been employed at the brewery next to the river Thames. The bottles of beer stretch back to the horizon.

the week-day meals of repetitive servings of meat and potatoes and bread and cheese, with occasional treats of a rasher or two of bacon or some sausages.

Where the wages of labourers were at their lowest – in the 1860s in the counties of Dorset, Kent, Chester, Salop, Stafford and Rutland – the diet might be as poor as bread and potatoes with an occasional bit of cheese. Bacon was a luxury, sometimes eaten raw. The poorest households could not even afford to buy tea, and a substitute was brewed by pouring hot water over burnt bread crusts.

In the middle of the nineteenth century, some rural working classes could supplement their diet with produce grown on allotments. The allocation of allotments was in response to the deprivations imposed on the poor by the Enclosure Acts, which progressively removed common land from use by the people at will. On allotments, or on small garden plots if they were lucky enough to have them, labourers could grow produce to eat themselves or to increase their incomes by the sale of fruit and vegetables such as gooseberries, strawberries, raspberries, black and red currants, apples, potatoes, French and runner beans and peas.

By the 1870s and 1880s, allotment plots were beginning to be carved out in the inner cities, too, providing somewhere for the

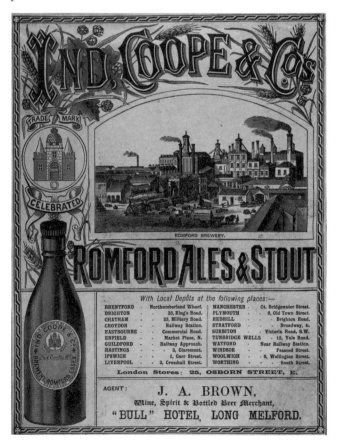

*An 1892 showcard lists Ind Coope's local depots (**left**). The view of the brewery in Romford, Essex dates back to a much earlier period, perhaps when it was first in operation. A flunky from an affluent household is sent out in a snowstorm for a supply of oatmeal stout (**above**), maybe required as urgent medicine for an invalid.*

poorer urban populations to grow healthy food. Victorian reformers promoted the practice, particularly those keen to keep the poor out of the public houses, sober and industrious on their own little pieces of land. An Allotment Act of 1887 proved partially successful in obliging local authorities to provide allotments where there was demand, but the movement really gathered pace in the early years of the twentieth century, underwritten by a more powerful and successful act of 1908. It is safe to say, though, that in the second half of the nineteenth century more urban working-class people were to be found spending their leisure time drinking in a public house, if and when they could afford to do so, than digging an allotment.

In rural areas it might be another tipple, such as cider, that quenched a thirst and lightened a mood. People were used to drinking in quantity, even coming to depend on it. An interesting passage from Cecil Torr's memoir *Small Talk at Wreyland*, about a Victorian Devonshire community, throws light on a level of drinking limited by the resources of the drinkers; it also casts doubt on the wisdom of a preference for tea:

> Men can easily get drunk on cider; but they do not suffer for it next day, if they have had pure cider of fermented apple-juice and nothing else.
>
> …A shrewd observer said to me:—'When each man had three pints of cider every day, there was not half this bickering and quarrelling that goes on now.' And that, I think, is true. They were always in a genial state of drunkenness, and seldom had the means of going beyond that.
>
> …On the whole, less harm is done by cider than by tea; but cider gets more blame, as its ill effects are visible at once, whereas tea works its mischief slowly.

Just what this mischief might be is not explained, but perhaps it is a reference to the tea addiction that the British of all classes are famous for, and to their apparent inability to act coherently without a top-up of the infusion.

The Victorians' serious interest in food and drink extended into every social pleasure and encounter in which it could play a part, whether in the warm conviviality of the public house or at a grand ball or banquet. Hotels, restaurants, refreshment rooms and supper rooms increased hugely in number in the second half of the nineteenth century, to cater for new patterns of work and social habits, and for new pockets full of money and opportunities for leisure. Pleasure gardens and parks, national celebrations of royal weddings and jubilees provided the potential for enjoyment to all but the penniless. Blanchard Jerrold observes Londoners at play in his Pilgrimage *of 1872, summing up in a few words an era of glitter and new excitements in the city:*

> We are now in the Music Hall and Refreshment Bar epoch: an epoch of much gilding and abundant looking-glass—as, on the stage, we are in the era of spangles and burlesque: as, at the Opera, we are in the age of the Traviata.

More genteel and restrained pleasures than those Jerrold describes were to be had at home, or on trips from home with friends, family and new acquaintances. Luncheons and afternoon teas, picnics, tennis and water parties, train excursions and beach outings were all opportunities for meeting, for intrigues and romances, and for eating and drinking. Eating and what you ate were important enjoyments. 'And, speaking of the science

A glass of lemonade is the ideal refreshment here at a tennis party. Plenty of fresh air was a preoccupation at the turn of the century; the imagined country house has a stone veranda and window flung open. The two young women are dressed in their smartest day wear and appear ill-prepared for any but the gentlest game of tennis.

*Drinkers at The Duke of Brunswick public house on New Cut, London (**right**) pose for the camera in an interior dimly lit by gas lights above the bar. This was one of thousands of local city pubs at the turn of the century that provided meeting places and recreation for working people who had little access to other ways of spending their leisure time.*

of Life, have you got the cucumber sandwiches cut for Lady Bracknell?' asks Algernon of his manservant in Oscar Wilde's *The Importance of Being Earnest* of 1895.

Nights out and evenings in

*In the days when trains stopped at stations long enough for passengers to stretch their legs or buy a snack, the boy in this advertisement (**left**) touts his delicious soft drinks. First-, second- and third-class travellers are depicted in characteristic dress, suggesting that the lemonade is an appropriate beverage for all.*

It was all too easy for Victorian social reformers to throw up their hands in horror at the proliferation of public houses and the drinking that was done there, but for many working-class people, in cities and rural towns and villages, the public house provided the only available social life and entertainment. This was usually the principal meeting place in a district (apart from church), where discussions could be had and, increasingly, clubs and societies could meet, perhaps in upstairs rooms designed for the purpose. Simple entertainment could be had in the form of pub games, such as bagatelle, darts and dominoes and, particularly in the late nineteenth century, billiards. Informal concerts provided cheering background to the conversation in modest pubs, and some city pubs had well organized musical

evenings to entertain the clientele. And that clientele, incidentally, was not confined only to the social class that had no other entertainment option; public houses could provide daring pleasures for middle-class men on the lookout for some excitement.

The public house increased in popularity as the attractions of the gin palace, frequented from early in the nineteenth century, began to wane. Gin palaces were under heavy criticism for the level of drunkenness and debauchery that they encouraged – again, of course, usually a reference to the assumed unbridled behaviour of the lower classes, voiced by their social superiors. A. Mearns and W.C. Preston, however, writing in the pamphlet *The Bitter Cry of Outcast London*, observe the scene in one of the many gin palaces of Leicester Square as late as October 1883 and take a more compassionate view about why people found them so magnetic:

> With its brightness, its excitement, and its
> temporary forgetfulness of misery, it is a
> comparative heaven to tens of thousands. How
> can they be expected to resist its temptations?
> They could not live if they did not drink, even
> though they know that by drinking they do
> worse than die.

Gin palaces were of gaudy but irresistible design

This poster (**opposite**) advertising a Tyneside brewery was published in 1898, but the gentleman farmer enjoying the malt stout in a country pub is dressed in Georgian garb, perhaps to give him a traditional and respectable air.

The bright lamp on the corner of a city public house (**above**), and the warm glow from inside, illustrate the irresistible attractions of such venues in the dark night streets. The partying spills outside, where women in their finery dance and the men watch. The engraving dates from 1890.

– bright lights shining out into the dingy streets, over-the-top architecture, chandeliers, great columns in a mishmash of classical styles to emulate the palaces of their title. Here was a bit of exoticism and light relief in a grey, hard environment, and a release from the mind- and body-numbing work of many a labourer's day. It was not just the attractions of the drink that were so compelling, but also the attractions of warmth, the inside, conviviality and glamour.

The later nineteenth-century public house inherited many elements of the gin palace's architectural style and there is sometimes confusion between them, with elaborately decorated public houses being called gin palaces as though the two were synonymous. Public house exteriors and interiors tended towards a pick-and-mix of the architectural styles popular at the time – Victorian Gothic, Classical Grecian, Italian palazzo. With firelight, oil lamps and, later, gas lights magnified by swathes of pretty bevelled glass glistening behind shiny mahogany bars, these interiors – as enticing as those of the gin palace, but more homely into the bargain – were on virtually every urban street corner and at the heart of every rural village. Other city public houses were much larger, cavernous beer-houses with musical entertainments that attracted many thousands of working people every week, such as those established in Manchester in the 1850s. Women were commonly seen drinking, too, even in the middle of the day, and by the 1890s some public houses had 'ladies only' rooms to accommodate the phenomenon of groups of female friends out for enjoyment.

A Victorian man out for the night with some

Men, women, children and dogs are all here in what appears to be a very functional drinking den in 1872. The lithograph contains a moral message: the top-hatted man continues to drink desperately, oblivious to the swooning drunkenness of a child in his care. The scene is observed by a well-dressed lady: a social reformer or philanthropist?

Serious drinking is also under way at this singing saloon in London's East End, drawn in 1871. Daringly dressed young women perform songs on the small stage and circulate among the audience. Music and singing made pubs and clubs very popular, particularly to those who could not afford more elaborate entertainments.

money to spend could take a fair pick of entertainment for the eye, the ear and the stomach on the streets of a city. Perhaps it would be a supper room to eat oysters and drink champagne, or to cavort with actresses and dancers at two or three in the morning over a meal of cold ham and fowl. *Punch* magazine describes such venues in 1842 as having for their object 'the promotion of social harmony and relief of domestic ennui', particularly when they include an entertainment of comic songs along with the beer, gin, whisky or brandy, the freshly prepared dishes of steak, eggs or broiled kidneys, and the luxury of cigars. Another piece in the magazine in 1856 wryly characterizes their attractions by suggesting that 'a glass of grog, with the accompaniment of good singing, may have a moral value superior to that of a teetotal harangue and a cup of Twankay'. Certainly, such places were a lot more attractive than the offerings of the temperance movement. At a club in London's Covent Garden piazza, for example, chops and potatoes 'never to be equalled' were to be had with 'all good drink', and nearby in Bow Street was one of the popular 'Judge and Jury Clubs', in which the burlesque was provided in an entertainment of a mock trial, the excuse both for filthy jokes and a filthy amount of drinking. The clubs were,

117

HALL & CO, LD.,
SYPHONS OF SODA WATER, POTASS WATER AND LEMONADE

LEMON SQUASH, FERMENTED GINGER BEER, HOP BITTERS, AND ALL High-class Aerated Table Waters of unexcelled BRILLIANCY, PURITY, AND STRENGTH.

Albion Aerated Water Works, NORTH SHIELDS.

according to an account from 1858, 'but an excuse for drinking'. 'If you wish to see your son thoroughly depraved,' it suggests, 'send him to a Judge and Jury Club. In a little while he will come back to you with every noble principle blotted out…'. No wonder foreign visitors, including a number of journalists, came to London expressly to witness the drunken debaucheries of the city, and that home-grown social reformers were so anxious to keep the tides threatening respectable lives at bay.

Evening entertainments that could be controlled, that were separated off from the mix of the urban streets and venues, were to be had at home. Much literature about the proper construction of parties at home was

Here are, perhaps, the origins of our taste for bottled fizzy drinks. Ginger beer is still popular, but other modern 'aerated' table waters, including a syphon of soda water, signal twentieth-century tastes.

Mrs Beeton's Household Management illustrates some complicated 'Cold Collation Dishes', which might provoke kitchen nerves. Expertise in making pie crusts and in the elaborate sculpting and garnishing of dishes were required to create these culinary masterpieces for a supper table.

published in promotion of such approved activity. In this way the pleasures and anxieties of the middle-class dinner party were carried through into other home entertaining – at private concerts, music parties and balls, for instance. In fact, these events could be even more ambitious and correspondingly terrifying. Mrs Beeton has detailed suggestions for menus for ball suppers for sixty guests, complete with table plans for the positioning of the dishes for guests to approach, buffet style. Her 'bill of fare' for a ball supper or 'cold collation' for a summer entertainment or a wedding or christening breakfast for seventy or eighty persons, for example, comes with the following note:

> The length of the page will not admit of our giving the dishes as they should be placed on the table; they should be arranged with the large and high dishes down the centre, and the spaces filled up with the smaller dishes, fruit, and flowers, taking care that the flavours and colours contrast nicely, and that no two dishes of a sort come together.

The suitable cold fare includes dishes of cut-up lobster, garnished tongue, raised pies, mayonnaise of salmon, blancmanges, cheesecakes, fruit tarts and jellies. Beeton assumes that the hostess will have on hand as a matter of course biscuits and wafers, cream-and-water, ices, tea, coffee, wines, liqueurs, soda water, ginger beer and lemonade. And all this is somehow to be designed so that it 'may be eaten standing without any trouble'. The 'Member of the Aristocracy' author of *Manners and Rules of Good Society* is quite clear about the refreshments to be served at such evening party occasions: 'Tea and light refreshments should be served during the evening in the library, or in an adjacent apartment. Supper

120   should be served at twelve o'clock in the dining-room…'. The Aristocrat makes no attempt to fudge the issue of how many and of what denomination were the rooms of the house, so his advice would pose something of a problem if your home did not have a library.

Articles and manuals advising on etiquette give clear and sometimes obvious directions as to proper behaviour on such occasions: 'Good taste dictates to most people that loud remarks and laughter are never more ill-timed than during the performance of music.' And of course women need to be particularly careful that their behaviour does not betray too much gusto at such occasions: 'The rustling of programmes and tapping of fans is the only applause ladies are supposed to bestow.' Beeton offers advice on the duties and demeanour of household staff. Attendants at evening card parties should move about actively and noiselessly to service the guests, and should not threaten concentration at a game of cribbage with the 'creaking of shoes, which is an abomination'. At a ball, which 'in all its parts … should be perfect', the lady of the house has literally to watch her step:

> It will be well for the hostess, even if she be very partial to the amusement, and a graceful dancer, not to participate in it to any great extent, lest her lady guests should have occasion to complain of her monopoly of the gentlemen, and other causes of neglect.

She might, though, have little strength left to dance after a build up to the ball that could include taking the doors of the house off their hinges and suspending muslin curtains instead, designing a cloakroom with numbered tickets and hiring additional candelabra for good illumination and cane chairs for sitting out round the dance floor. Balls were not for the domestically fainthearted.

A priest is sorely tempted to a tot of whisky at a railway buffet, although his own particular etiquette would counsel against. The brand offered by the lonely barmaid could prove irresistible in this advertisement, which is typical of those of the turn-of-the-century period in its gentle humour.

Days out

Mrs Beeton provides a useful little section in her *Book of Household Management* about things that should not be forgotten at a picnic. They are: 'A stick of horseradish, a bottle of mint-sauce well corked, a bottle of salad dressing, a bottle of vinegar, made mustard, pepper, salt, good oil, and pounded sugar.' This is picnicking in style. The food might be cold roast beef, ribs and shoulders of lamb, fowl and duck, ham, tongue, meat pies, lobsters, lettuces and cucumbers. Stewed fruit can be taken in glass bottles with biscuits to eat alongside, there should be fresh fruit and pastries – and even blancmanges wobbled their way along in moulds to be consumed in the great open air. The appropriate quantities of alcoholic drinks, according to Beeton, for a picnic for forty, are three dozen quart bottles of ale, six bottles of sherry, six bottles of claret, champagne '*à discrétion*' and other light wine, and two bottles of brandy.

The choice of location for a picnic, and the way in which guests were to be transported there, took a degree of planning. The most reliable choice of site would be one advised by the landlord of a local inn or hotel; he

Huntley & Palmer's inventive biscuit trade card of about 1880 owes something in spirit, perhaps, to Manet's celebrated painting Déjeuner sur l'herbe of 1863 – although at this respectable luncheon party the women are fully clothed and the venue is Epping Forest, east of London.

A picnic is laid out on the beach at Kennack Sands in Cornwall at the turn of the century. This is quite a large party, which could be from a local village church or another institution that was keen to record the day's fun on film.

could then be employed to provide the necessary drink and crockery and cutlery, and even to deliver all the food if desired. His inn or hotel would also conveniently provide a place of refuge in case of bad weather. The location should ideally be near to a railway line, so that a carriage on a train could be hired in its entirety for the party of picnic guests to travel easily and in privacy on their day out. The whole enterprise was complicated, and in some cases was organized by a committee devised for the occasion and drawn from the invitees, particularly if the cost and sourcing of the food and drink were to be split between participants. Somebody would have to plan the transport of the food, possibly by separate tradesman's cart, making sure to acquire and correctly distribute ice under the supplies to keep perishable foods fresh on the journey. One manual of the 1880s has some clever advice for the transport of butter to the picnic site, that of gouging out the centre of fresh bread rolls and filling them with the butter. The split halves of the rolls then take on the duty of butter dishes when the picnic is laid out, as butter, 'when removed from the rolls, does not look inviting'. Even when all is arranged and the picnic is in full swing, the dangers and organization are not over, this manual cautions:

124 A picnic party occasionally attracts a good many loungers and lookers-on of a doubtful class. The only way to prevent these people from encroaching in dangerous proximity to the plate, &c., is to secure the attendance of a police officer in the grounds, within easy call, if not in sight.

Even the police officer is considered a servant to the occasion, better out of sight, and employed 'on payment of a trifle'. Any leftover food, it says, should be distributed amongst the poor – although not directly but ideally through the services of a lodgekeeper from the estate where the picnic has taken place, who will be 'the best medium for this description of gift'. Members of the middle-class party would not, after all, want to spoil their day out by themselves coming face to face with distressing poverty.

If not the very poor, at least a good number of social inferiors enjoyed their own picnics, less elaborate but more relaxed affairs, perhaps on farmland, at the beach or on a day out to a fair or a park. While some nineteenth-century paintings depict sentimentalized scenes of rosy-cheeked agricultural workers picnicking in the fields (when, in fact, those people would most likely have been far from pictures of health), photographs from later in the century show simple picnics, a tablecloth pinioned to the ground or on the beach, and large groups of family and friends clearly having a great day out.

In the cities, parks provided a place to promenade and breathe fresh air, to have a day or a few hours out and sample some treats along the way. Vauxhall Gardens, for example, were built over the main railway line to Victoria in 1859. Vauxhall Park, near the railway station in South Lambeth, was finally secured as parkland for the people in 1890 after years of lobby-

Sweet pies, puddings and pancakes, tarts, charlottes and dumplings were substantial desserts to return home to after a day out in the fresh air. Commonly grown fruits – apple, pear, cherry and apricot – are used in a variety of easily manageable recipes and are presented with the continental touch of a dish of olives.

ing by a cross-section of people from all classes. A letter to a national newspaper in the year of its opening declared that it

> …will form one of those all too few central gardens to which the very young and the very old, the over-worked in brief intervals of work, the convalescent, and the quite poor may find near to their own houses the rest, the air, the outside peace they so often need.

And where the people went for their moments of rest, the food stalls followed, selling similar fare to that found on the streets of the city – full-blown meals and, particularly, refreshing treats such as lemonade, ginger beer and ices. Hyde Park, in close proximity to the richest areas of London, was rather grander, a place 'where the upper classes of London congregate in the evening between five and seven o'clock, partly to take the air, and partly because it is considered fashionable to see now and then in order to be seen.' There was fun to be had there, though – skating on the Serpentine in winter, boating and horse riding. Swimming in the Serpentine was commonly pursued, but was not to be recommended, as the water was filthy, spattered with dead fish.

Eating, and particularly drinking, made up a large part of any communal celebration: Queen Victoria's Golden Jubilee of 1887 and her Diamond Jubilee of 1897 (even her funeral in 1901) were all opportunities for pageantry and partying on the streets. Contemporary observers seem to have been disappointed by the meagre spectacle of the Lord

The sumptuous picnic here is in Dunedin, New Zealand in the 1890s and picnickers are dressed up in their finest daywear. The feast and its accoutrements have been delivered to the spot by hand-cart. Young men scramble up a rock for some celebratory drinking.

126 Mayor's Show, on the other hand, although the guests at his sumptuous banquet might have thought differently. One guest described the meal served in 1895 as a 'modern dinner [which] may be described as a super-structure of the most elegant and artistic cookery, resting, however, on amazingly strong pillars of cold roast beef'. The influence of delicate French cookery had not, even by the end of the century, eroded the solid virtues of British staple fare. The same correspondent also attended a banquet given by the Worshipful Company of Fishmongers in the same year, and found the eating patterns there less than graceful:

> That most disastrous personage, the glutton, is generally taciturn at table. He eats, or rather he 'stokes' his meal, till the veins in his forehead swell, and his eyes grow glassy, and he breathes hard. You prefer the people with moderate appetites, who laugh and jest as they feast.

Riotous fun – and riots – could be had at country fairs. John Dunlop, writing about mid-century drinking habits in 1844, analyses Donnybrook Fair in the suburbs of Dublin. Such a fair is, he says, 'a kind of popular festival' at which there is 'wild tumult'. At Donnybrook, two to three hundred tents were pitched, the ground boarded up for dancing to the tune of fiddlers, and the revellers fuelled by a great deal of whiskey brought there from the surrounding public houses. As a result, Dunlop finds that a large proportion of the 'lower classes' are in a state of extreme drunkenness. Women are smoking, screaming and shouting;

The caption of this advertisement for lager refers to the tenacity of the two British hunting dogs, a bulldog and a terrier, flanking the bottle. The Scottish firm J. & R. Tennent was one of the first in Britain to brew the new lager beer.

The sort of fare that might go well with a bottle of beer is accurately drawn here. The quality of the pork pie is suggested by its delicious crust, and even the sausages are proudly displayed on plates with lace doilies.

some revellers are in such a state of inebriation that they lie on the damp ground all night and as a result, he says, catch all manner of diseases. His most extravagant claim for the consequences of such bad behaviour is that one man lying dead drunk on the ground for the night almost had his face eaten off by a pig.

The popular St Giles's Fair, held annually in Oxford as a holiday for working, people grew in size in the second half of the nineteenth century as a new band of revellers were brought into the city by rail. The Great Western Railway Company ran a special excursion train from Banbury to Oxford, stopping at stations along the way, in 1850. By the 1830s drinking and dancing booths were already in evidence at St Giles, and in the 1870s public houses in the city were granted permission to place drinking saloons on the street outside their premises during the fair. There were temperance refreshment tents, too, supplying tea and coffee. A great number of food stalls lined St Giles and its surrounding streets – selling sweets,

gingerbread and cakes. Street barrows had 'cocoa-nuts', hedge nuts and fruit on offer. Every year there were complaints about rowdy behaviour.

Blanchard Jerrold, in his *London: A Pilgrimage* of 1872, makes similarly disapproving noises about days out by Londoners: 'It is because their feasts are few and far between that we see "the violent delights" in which they indulge by the banks of the Thames at Easter, and on the Epsom Downs in May.' The event on Epsom Downs in May was the Derby, where Jerrold saw 'great refreshment booths' catering to the crowds. Even the journey to the Derby is an opportunity to get thoroughly in the mood:

> We admit that the halt at the road-side public house falls naturally into a
> very English scene. Pots of beer flash through the crowd: are lifted to the
> roofs of omnibuses, passed inside through the windows, raised to the lips of
> ladies who are giggling in spring carts, handed to postillions who drink
> while their horses plunge; and not an unwilling lip is seen anywhere.

From the 1860s, there was a great increase in the numbers, variety and configuration of places to eat out, from the restaurants of the new and fashionable hotels and attached to theatres, to luncheon bars and stunning new refreshment rooms at railway stations. The interiors could be magnificent, hung with chandeliers, glittering with gold leaf in the French style, and with small tables providing opportunities for daring new encounters – men and women dining in public together. Simpson's restaurant in the Strand was established in 1848, the Café Royale opened in 1865, the same year as the Langham Hotel, and the Criterion Restaurant and theatre was established by 1874. The year before, the St Pancras Hotel had

*Gustave Doré's detailed drawing of The Derby (**opposite**) to illustrate Jerrold's Pilgrimage records the excitement of a day at the races. Lunch is served in carriages – and even on top of them – while serious punters have binoculars at the ready and bets are placed.*

*Another important date in the social calendar (**below**) is Henley Regatta on the Thames. Members of the upper classes, with their parasols and striped blazers, are served a picnic by a maid on her hands and knees, while they dispense charity.*

opened to cater for train travellers, and boasted a magnificent coffee room of a completely different order and opulence from the dingy coffee shops of the inner city. The expanding choice of eating places extended to the sorts of cuisine on offer, too, with ethnic restaurants set up by immigrant communities in the areas in which they had become established. There were Italian restaurants in Holborn and Clerkenwell and French restaurants in Soho, where such exotic foods as garlic and olives could be tasted.

Tabitha Tickletooth makes quite an investigation of London restaurants in *The Dinner Question* of 1860. 'By slow degrees,' she points out, '"John

*Worcestershire sauce (**opposite**) came onto the market in the 1840s after, it is said, a chemist in Worcester mistakenly left a barrel of spiced vinegar to ferment but found the result tasty.*

*The Tivoli Music Hall opened on the Strand, London in May 1890. This poster for the Tivoli Restaurant (**above**) is in the style of Henri Toulouse-Lautrec, celebrated creator of posters for Parisian cabarets and cafes at the time. An association with the chic and fashionable was clearly in mind.*

Bull" became sobered down, and was well content to swallow some of his anti-Gallican prejudices, and a succulent French dinner at the same time.' She regrets, though, that we are behind the French in matters of taste, simply making a display of dishes that purport to be French but are unrecognizable as such. She finds the cheapest good dinner in London at Simpson's: their fish dinner for eighteen pence. The Wellington in St James's Street is for the wealthy and discerning, with a descending grade of menus – à la carte, French dinner, English dinner and the two-shilling 'joint and vegetables' – that makes clear the fashionable preference for French over English food. She recommends coffee dinners at the restaurant next to the Haymarket theatre and chop suppers under the piazza at Covent Garden, where superior musical entertainment nightly draws 'crowds of the best company in town'.

As the century progressed, eating out, in a commercial establishment and in public, had become respectable, not just for the working man but for all classes and, importantly, both genders. Women eating lunch out, or taking tea, or gracing refreshment rooms, were becoming an increasingly common and acceptable sight. In the evening, it would not be out of the question for a young lady to take dinner with a gentleman who was not her father or husband. Even modest meals could be delicious bargains. Molly Hughes describes one such, eaten with her mother while on holiday in Clacton in 1884:

> We were told that we could have the 'Farmers' Ordinary', and were given seats at a table with a sort of cloth laid. As it was rather late we were the only customers, and almost immediately there was brought a plate of food

each. I had no idea the Potteries made such enormous plates. Even so, the huge slices of beef fell over the edge. Potatoes, cabbage, and Yorkshire pudding were ranged around in decent plenty, while the whole was awash with rich gravy… What was our astonishment to find the charge only 1od. each.

At the same time as Molly Hughes and her mother relished their modest but generous dinner, some better-heeled diners were eating the most glamorous meals on the move. These were served against a changing backdrop of foreign cities, countryside and mountains and, eventually, the first glimpses of a mysterious Eastern world. The Orient Express train made its inaugural journey from the Gare de Strasbourg in Paris to Constantinople, modern-day Istanbul, on 4 October 1883. The journey took passengers through Strasbourg, Munich, Vienna, Budapest, Bucharest and Giurgiu, where a ferry crossed the Danube to Bulgaria, another train connected to Varna on the Black Sea and, finally, a steam ship took passengers on the voyage to

Gentlemen at their very grand club are drinking a suitably named whisky in this 1900 advertisement. Full evening dress, sculptural moustaches and a highly polished table all contribute to the high-class image courted for the whisky.

Constantinople. The dining car was beautiful, lit by gas lamps that glinted off the silverware and champagne glasses, and meals were served by an elite staff. All meals were cooked on board, using fresh ingredients taken in en route, and some dishes also conformed to those typical of the countries on the journey. It is said that the food was so good that people would board the Orient Express with the sole purpose of eating, only to get off at the next stop once the meal was finished.

Days at home

The lateness of the dinner hour in middle-class households – timed to accommodate the hours of business and return of the men of the house – resulted in an emphasis on a new meal, as our Aristocrat was quick to point out towards the end of the nineteenth century in editions of *Manners and Rules of Good Society*:

Such was the interior, the furnishings, the tablewares and the food in the Orient Express restaurant car that this engraving was made during the first months of its run in 1883. The railway carriage has been transformed into miniature ballroom, complete with ceiling mouldings and chandelier.

> Invitations to luncheon are very much the order of the day in fashionable society. Those who look back some few years, remark the importance now accorded to this mid-day meal, and contrast it with the past.

Luncheon provided opportunities for new social gatherings, ones with a lightness of touch, planned for uncomplicated amusement and free from some of the stresses of entertaining dinner guests with business advancement in mind. As an etiquette manual of the 1880s puts it: 'Each year, as the hour of dinner becomes later, luncheons increase in favour, and afford opportunities of receiving visitors in the most cordial and unrestrained manner.' Luncheon at home was by and large the preserve of women while

134 men were otherwise occupied, apart from the possibility of 'the presence of the unemployed and youthful male members of the family'. Even then, the etiquette manual suggests that these men might eat at table but then make themselves scarce, and that servants be dismissed after serving the main course, creating a delicious new opportunity for women to talk together free of the constraints imposed by men's expectations. Paradoxically, women's new freedom here was provoked by contemporary mores, which frowned upon ladies inviting men outside the immediate family to luncheon when their husbands were not present. The meal was timed at about two o'clock in town, half an hour or so earlier in the country. It could be comparatively simple, relying chiefly on cold joints of meat and fresh fruits or simple tarts, but would not preclude alcohol. Women drinking at luncheons, wine and liqueurs or beer, is commented upon with a mixture of surprise, disapproval and perhaps a tinge of fear in contemporary writing about fashionable society. Who could say what these women would be talking and laughing about?

The important new luncheon meal also gave scope for some more elaborate fun, arranged around lawn tennis, archery, cricket matches or bazaars at the grandest places, or as a smaller town garden party, where croquet may have been the game of choice. Garden parties 'are especially suited to inhabitants of suburban villas', we are told, although their rise in popularity was

Fashionable afternoon tea is here taken out with the children in Regent Street, London in 1893. A little girl is choosing her cakes from a plentiful display at the counter. By the end of the century, teatime was another opportunity for comparatively informal social encounters.

AFTERNOON TEA IN REGENT STREET
DRAWN BY MARY L. GOW, R.I.

The poster advertising lemonade from which the detail on page 111 is taken suggests that the young gentleman entertaining the ladies here is a sporty student, as he is dressed in Cambridge university's light blue and is, after all, hosting a tennis party.

promoted by the more elevated new habits of Queen Victoria, who had a preference for such occasions. Menus and their presentation were dictated by the complexities of eating outside in a British climate. Tea, coffee, biscuits, sandwiches, strawberries and cream and ices were the order of the garden party. It was not wise to have all the refreshments presented out of doors, though, unless you had recourse to a marquee, as there could be an undignified scramble in a case of bad weather. Better to have just some of the most attractive dishes outside because then, as *Manners and Rules* suggests, 'should heavy rain set in, the servants can easily remove pails of ice and bowls of strawberries out of harm's way'.

Garden parties were considered one variation of an 'at home', a term used to cover the panoply of domestic entertaining, from tea parties to balls. At their simplest, 'at homes' could entail the hostess remaining in her drawing room on a particular day to receive visitors, and serving light refreshments to those who arrived. As guests might spend a very short time in any one household, taking in a number of open houses in an afternoon, the refreshments did not need to be elaborate. The conventions of the tea party were still popular, where guests were invited between the hours of about four and seven and served in the drawing room with tea and delicate sandwiches, bread and butter and simple cakes, by servants. This is the environment in which Lady Bracknell would have eaten her cucumber sandwiches had they not all been scoffed before her arrival in Wilde's *The Importance of Being Earnest*:

136 LADY BRACKNELL: I'm sorry if we are a little late, Algernon, but I was
obliged to call on dear Lady Harbury. I hadn't been there since her poor
husband's death. I never saw a woman so altered; she looks quite twenty
years younger. And now I'll have a cup of tea, and one of those nice
cucumber sandwiches you promised me.

ALGERNON: Certainly, Aunt Augusta. [*Goes over to tea-table.*]

LADY BRACKNELL: Won't you come and sit here, Gwendolen?

GWENDOLEN: Thanks, mamma, I'm quite comfortable where I am.

ALGERNON: [*Picking up empty plate in horror.*] Good heavens! Lane! Why
are there no cucumber sandwiches? I ordered them specially.

LANE: [*Gravely.*] There were no cucumbers in the market this morning, sir.
I went down twice.

ALGERNON: No cucumbers!

LANE: No, sir. Not even for ready money.

The opportunity for afternoon guests to come and go, visiting without great
obligation and without too much significance placed on each attendance, created a fluidity through which, for example, young men could visit the houses of young women of their mere acquaintance with the prospect then of cultivating further encounters. Inviting guests to tea had other advantages of economy of time and money. The 1880s manual comments that 'many persons, who have neither the inclination nor the means to give set dinners, sometimes make the partak-

Afternoon tea simply would not be worthy of the name without cakes, allowing plenty of scope for the plethora of late nineteenth- and early twentieth-century manufacturers of cakes, cakes mixes and baking powders. The use of children, and often animals, in food advertising campaigns emphasizes the warmth and homeliness of the products.

Afternoon tea is served at a lawn tennis tournament in 1892. Household furniture and household servants are brought outside to service the guests; and the social, rather than the sporting, opportunities of the occasion are most in evidence.

ing of the favourite beverage an occasion for seeing friends in an unceremonious manner.' Tea-time could also be an open-ended affair, filling the long and otherwise boring stretch between lunch and a late dinner hour for those with nothing more constructive to do.

The Victorian enthusiasm for home and family naturally extended entertaining to the children, whose parties, birthday or otherwise, were given with a new informality that gave real consideration to amusements that the children would actually enjoy. Party games such as 'hunt the slipper' or 'blind man's buff' were popular, and entertainers such as conjurers might be hired for the occasion. Recommended foods were homemade confectioneries, pastries, sandwiches and sponge cake, and beverages included lemonade, orange and cherryade, and 'orgeat', a barley water. At different times of the year other children's party pleasures were thought appropriate,

138 such as Easter Nests, when little wicker or cardboard baskets full of stained or painted hard-boiled eggs could be secreted around the garden or out in the woods for the children to find.

The festive occasion most strongly associated with all that is characterized as Victorian – home and hearth, attachment to family ideals, rich food and drink, elaborate decoration – is undoubtedly Christmas. The traditions to which we adhere today at Christmas were in large part dreamed up or introduced to Britain in the middle of the nineteenth century. The sending of Christmas cards, for example, was made possible by a widespread postal service transported by rail. It appealed to those split from their families by the necessity of a move to industrial towns and cities. Food and drink were the most crucial elements of a successful Victorian Christmas; even the most modest of households would prepare and stock up on what provisions it could. The delicious treats to eat and drink were brought out ceremoniously at Christmas dinners, a ritual that fast became powerfully familiar. In *Great Expectations* (1861) Dickens uses the symbolic power of a single item of Christmas food to great effect. Contemporaneous readers would have trembled in fearful anticipation of what would happen to the boy Pip when his theft of a magnificent pork pie, which he has stolen for the convict Magwitch, is discovered:

> I stole some bread, some rind of cheese, about half a jar of mincemeat (which I tied up in my pocket-handkerchief with my last night's slice), some brandy from a stone bottle (which I decanted into a glass bottle I had secretly used for

A Christmas bowl of punch is mixed by a coachman and served to a huntsman and an elderly woman, in this 1880s magazine image. Mrs Beeton says of punch: 'It is considered to be very intoxicating; but this is probably because the spirit, being partly sheathed by the mucilaginous juice and the sugar, its strength does not appear to the taste so great as it really is.'

The Coachman mixes a Christmas Bowl
(The Huntsman is exceedingly fond of Punch.)

A Christmas pudding aflame is triumphantly delivered to the table in the 1894 painting Christmas Comes But Once a Year *by Charles Green. Diners in their satins and silks, a young boy in velvet suit and servants in freshly laundered uniforms are dressed in their traditional best, but the table is quite spartan and modern in style.*

making that intoxicating fluid, Spanish-liquorice-water, up in my room; diluting the stone bottle from a jug in the kitchen cupboard), a meat bone with very little on it, and a beautiful round compact pork pie. I was nearly going away without the pie, but I was tempted to mount upon a shelf, to look what it was that was put away so carefully in a covered earthenware dish in a corner, and I found it was the pie, and I took it, in the hope that it was not intended for early use, and would not be missed for some time.

The terrified child Pip, anxious to avoid the murderous threats of Magwitch and the vicious wrath of the elder sister in whose house he lives, remains unaware of the social and ritual significance of the pork pie until the Christmas meal for which it was intended, when all becomes sickeningly clear to him.

140

'You must taste,' said my sister, addressing the guests with her best grace, 'you must taste, to finish with, such a delightful and delicious present of Uncle Pumblechook's!'

Must they! Let them not hope to taste it!

'You must know,' said my sister, rising, 'it's a pie: a savoury pork pie.'

In *Household Management* Mrs Beeton points to the symbolism of another item of the Christmas table, the turkey. A single sentence describing the importance of this fowl contains many clues to Victorian preoccupations – in its references to empire, to the envy that an ideal family with ideal food on its table could hope to inspire, to the well-fed head of the family and to the requirements of charity:

A Christmas dinner, with the middle classes of this empire, would scarcely be a Christmas dinner without its turkey; and we can hardly imagine an object of greater envy than is presented by a respected portly paterfamilias carving, at the season devoted to good cheer and genial charity, his own fat turkey, and carving it well.

The passage does beg the question, though, as to how purposefully Beeton parallels the corpulent father and the corpulent fowl. In the pages of Beeton we find recipes for Christmas foods that we still use routinely today. Plum (Christmas) pudding is made with suet, soft sugar, raisins, currants, sultanas, candied peel, lemon rind, nutmeg and cinnamon, with a good quarter pint of brandy. There is an 'Excellent Mincemeat' made with plenty of

Wrapped up against the cold of a Scottish winter, a happy crew bring home the prize of a very large bottle of whisky. The poster's rural, horse-and-coaches, old-fashioned air is synonymous with the traditional Christmas cheer invented by the Victorians.

apple, lemon zest and orange marmalade. She has recipes for bread sauce, for sausage meat stuffing and for a brandy sauce for the pudding.

Some were less than sanguine about the celebratory opportunities offered by a family Christmas. Writing in 1844, John Dunlop comments on the frivolous dispensing of drink to all and sundry at Christmas. On a day of 'good cheer', he says, callers to the home expect to be served with plum bread, cheese and beer and spirits as a matter of course. Servants often receive their 'Christmas box' with a glass of gin, and then decamp to the public house to spend the 'box' on further intoxicating liquor. Worst of all, children often get their first taste of drink as they go from house to house wishing everyone a Happy Christmas, as beer, he says, is put to their lips for the amusement of the adults; this becomes an 'initiation of young people into the practice of intemperance'. The whole occasion is one in which the upper and middle classes are involved in 'free drinking'.

Comic illustrator John Leech published this image on New Year's Day 1900; it is captioned 'Fetching Home the Christmas Dinner'. London's poorer classes are collecting their cooked Christmas meals from the ovens of the baker (called 'J. Rusk'), while street children capitalize on the season of good will and charity.

For many, though, Christmas was an occasion of unusual merriment, and of eating and drinking that they could not in any case afford during the rest of the year. It was one day off, at least. Poorer city residents hoped to have saved enough to take away a hot Christmas dinner from the cookshop, to have a drink with friends, or to benefit from a season of charity that might just fall their way. The middle classes, meanwhile, were happy to enjoy a few days of well-earned leisure in the pursuit of family unity and a jolly good, home-cooked meal.

*A*s the nineteenth century drew to a close, the pioneering, self-improving sense of purpose that had characterized the British earlier in Victoria's reign became somewhat diluted. Many felt a weight of duty to achieve respectability, to demonstrate accomplishments – amongst them the culinary, dinner-giving sort – lift from their shoulders. Preoccupations became more light-hearted, frivolous even, and tastes, if they could be afforded, were for the exotic, the satirical, the continental. Some strengths of the earlier Victorian character were sacrificed, perhaps, in favour of easier enjoyments, but with them at least went some of the dispiriting shackles of religion and propriety that restricted behaviour earlier in the century. People embraced instead a more secular and scientific age (one by now quite accustomed to Darwin's mid-century theories of evolution) – and an increasingly democratic one that involved greater numbers of its people in education and relative prosperity. Even so, the affluent or reasonably affluent late Victorian, and certainly the Edwardian in the first decade of the twentieth century, had a tendency to crave personal excitement rather than democratic accountability. An ease of living and the enjoyment of amenities were the aspirations and, for some Edwardians, leisure pursuits were very flash and dilettante indeed.

By 1911, the date of this poster, whisky and soda was so fashionable that stylish gentlemen would be unlikely to drink their scotch neat. The soda syphon was to retain its pride of place on the drinks tray for at least another half century.

"A parting Nip of the Finest."

Domestic bliss

The scientific advances of the nineteenth century meant that by its end, and in the first decade or so of the twentieth, labour in the home, and particularly in the kitchen, began to be eased by newfangled technologies and gadgets. A modern middle-class kitchen could be equipped with devices to mince meat and peel potatoes and, crucially from the point of view of diet and domestic routine, by 1900 a quarter of urban households had a gas cooker. This constant source of instant cooking fuel revolutionized the lives of many mistresses of the house and their servants. A refrigerator was no longer out of the question, although it was not yet an electric one: the cabinet had a pair of compartments, one to house a block of ice and another in which to store the food. This refrigerator may have been basic, but nevertheless it was a fantastic boon for some lucky housewives: the ability to

This proposed setting for a tea table is taken from a 1907 edition of Mrs Beeton's Household Management, which bore very little resemblance to Isabella's original 1861 work. The table design has an Edwardian daintiness and the tableware a made-for-the-purpose delicacy.

Four young women take tea together in 1908. Their table is as overflowing with modern garden flower arrangements as that in the suggested design opposite, and they use a similar mix of china and silver-plate wares. The sideboard behind them is of a contemporary Arts and Crafts style; its clean lines and lack of clutter mark it apart from nineteenth-century equivalents.

store fresh produce meant fewer shopping excursions. Although poverty, poor housing and poor sanitation still plagued a large proportion of the population, who even now had recourse to nothing more than hard domestic slog, simple homemaking was increasingly big business, of serious interest to greater numbers of people. By 1908, the *Daily Mail* Ideal Home Exhibition opened for the first time at Olympia to showcase the modern home, the same year in which Hoover patented the first electric carpet-sweeper. The electric kettle, with its element on the outside, existed from the beginning of the twentieth century – but such goods were an unimaginable luxury for all but the wealthy.

The photographs of that first Ideal Home Exhibition which still exist

*The Cadbury's Cocoa advertisement back on page 46 gave recipes for making the drink, but here detailed instructions are no longer necessary now cocoa is well established (**above**). Instead, the nutritional value of the product is tracked through the three ages of man and compared favourably to that of other common foods.*

*Bacon and eggs or ham and eggs are so popular as dishes with which to start the day that this advertisement (**left**) refers specifically to breakfast. The Edwardian butcher appears younger and slimmer than his Victorian promotional counterpart.*

show stands festooned with advertisements by manufacturing companies producing goods of one sort or another for the home (those companies who would presumably also advertise in the *Daily Mail* newspaper). Amongst the advertisements for soap and other cleaning materials are many for processed and packaged foods, from J.S. Fry and Sons chocolate to Bird's custard, now firmly established in British households. Although these products that had first stormed the markets in the 1870s and 1880s had the most secure hold at the start of twentieth century, they were by now in increasing competition with many others. The Liebig Company's extract of beef, for example, was renamed Oxo in 1900 and widely marketed. Domestic magazines, and others aimed at women, such as fiction magazines, now carried pages of small advertisements for all sorts of widely available packaged foods. There were 'grape-nuts' made from wheat and barley and 'rich in the elements required for human nourishment'. The early equivalent of the late twentieth-century 'cup-a-soup', Edwards' Desiccated Soup, to which the housewife could add hot water or use to bulk out an existing homemade broth, 'imparts thickness, nourishment and colour'. There were advertisements for digestive biscuits, tomato catsup (ketchup), yeast, cane sugar, Swiss milk chocolate, Cakeoma (a pudding and cake mix), lemon cheese (lemon curd) – all sorts of fabulous additions to the larder. Digestive systems were still something of an obsession, though, with advertisements for Henry's Calcined Magnesia for Heartburn, Headache, Gout, Biliousness, or Acidity of the Stomach and Whelpton's Purifying Pills for Indigestion, for example, interspersed with

148 the food advertisements. Some of these companies also began to advertise more glamorously elsewhere: from the 1890s 'electric' advertisements had started to go up in Trafalgar Square, and then in Piccadilly Circus.

Many of these processed food products were now routinely found in even quite modest larders, and not just in towns but in rural areas, too, as distribution networks penetrated further afield. A study of a village in Wiltshire made in 1909, for example, finds the diet of the family of a labourer based on a subsistence of tea, sugar, butter, bacon, cheese, lard, suet, oranges, currants and beer, but also containing Quaker oats (porridge was by now a staple breakfast for many), Fry's cocoa, and egg powder. This was still a very limited diet. Other reports on farm labourers' diets talk of rough tea made strong and drinkable by the addition of a lot of sugar, and a staple of potatoes crushed into gravy as a main meal. But such repetitive eating could be cheered by the treat of tinned herrings, sardines or even salmon now and again, indicating that packaged foods were of enormous importance to poor families.

The contents of Edwardian recipe books illustrate an assumption that convenience products, such as baking powder and gelatin, would be at all the readers' fingertips. And many of the standard recipes that used them are still familiar now: for almond biscuits, rock buns and ginger cake, for example. However, the number of jelly recipes – apricot, claret, Maraschino, Noyau, orange, raspberry, rhubarb, rum, sherry, strawberry, and wine in one such book – that employed the

Some of 'the lightest and daintiest biscuits made' float away like bubbles. In response to the worrying state of health of much of the population, the new twentieth century saw an increased concern with diet. These lightweight biscuits should be much easier on the digestion.

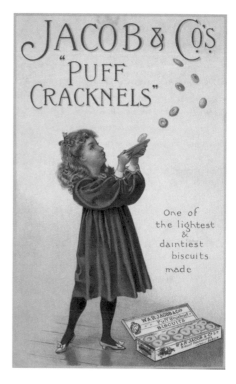

ICES
Prepared from
MERRILLS' Ice Cream Mixture
OR CUSTARD
ARE DELICIOUS

Edwardian ladies give the languorous air of having infinite leisure time as they wait for their refreshing ices to be served. They are drawn against a perfect, grand suburban setting of open rolling lawns and new-build, mock-Tudor house, complete with veranda. Such house designs were very much in vogue at the Daily Mail Ideal Home Exhibition in 1910.

miraculous powdered gelatin is certainly larger than it would be in a twenty-first-century equivalent. It is also clear to see by a flick through an Edwardian cookery book that afternoon tea was still a serious meal. Recipes for many different kinds of scone – brown, white, buttermilk, potato, soda, sago, milk – many different teacakes – American, Irish, Shrewsbury, Watford, Yorkshire – and also for quantities of crumpets, baps, gaufres, pikelets and waffles are testimony to the enduring importance of afternoon tea.

Domestic bliss on a grander Edwardian scale took place in lighter, airier interiors that had thrown off some of the Victorian clutter, at last taking heed of Charles Eastlake's advice in a bid for modernity and lightness of style. Pastel floral wallpapers and upholstery, at their most fashionable edge perhaps in leaf green, lilac and grey, replaced the dark greens and reds and browns of the previous century. The Victorian interior had been weeded out to a thinner style, a sort of neo-Georgian look that seemed much more confident and elegant. Or it may have adopted one of the other lighter or more exotic styles that were the height of fashion at the time. The Arts and Crafts Movement espoused a return to a simple, vernacular style characterized by its fitness for use, rather than its decorative appeal. Meanwhile, members of the Aesthetic Movement in art and interiors had reacted against dour utilitarianism in favour of creating beauty for its own, unencumbered sake. The French Art Nouveau style, with its sinuous, stylized plants, decorated simpler fixtures and fittings, such as fireplaces, tiles and stained glass. In their different ways, each of these styles modified the Victorian interior to a comparative simplicity, but often an expensive simplicity nevertheless. The principles of the new looks, though, provided inspiration for the architecture and interiors of the new suburbs of the period, particularly in the garden cities. The first was at Letchworth in Hertfordshire, built in 1903 and providing a range of housing, from larger detached dwellings to terraced cottages.

In the grander of these middle-class environments, tea and toast or bread and butter would be served in the bedrooms, then servants would continue their daily toil to produce breakfast, lunch and dinner – interrupted, of course, by afternoon tea – for the family of the house. Dinner parties were not quite as elaborate as they had been in the nineteenth century and were restricted to about eight or ten dishes, rather than the twenty or so required in pre-

After the annual Oxford versus Cambridge University Boat Race on the Thames, sporting young men celebrate with dubious young women, who appear to be cavorting and propositioning in a manner less than ladylike.

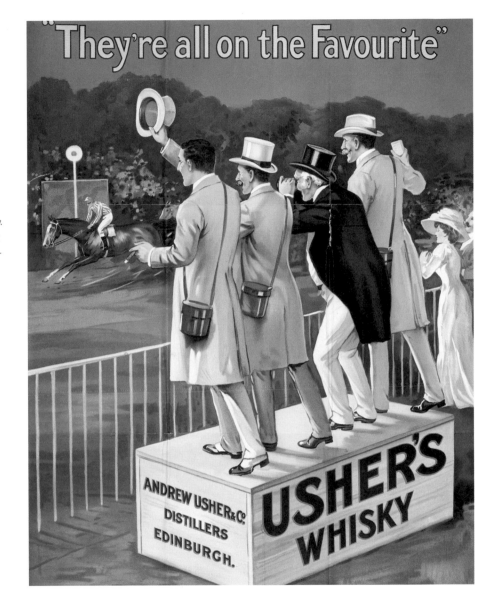

"They're all on the Favourite"

ANDREW USHER & C?
DISTILLERS
EDINBURGH.

USHER'S WHISKY

Sporting events were above all social occasions. These four men have backed the same winning horse and are about to celebrate with a particular brand of whisky. Although whisky was drunk by all classes, this advertisement is true to form in identifying the brand with members of the upper echelons.

vious decades. Even so, for ordinary affairs dishes could still include lobster bisque, pheasant in aspic, quails, rabbit and grouse. And the rigmarole of fine china, glass and silver, of the correct attendance of servants, and of the etiquette of dining was even more exacting. Meanwhile, beer was still served at all servants' meals, which were taken with a formality imitative of

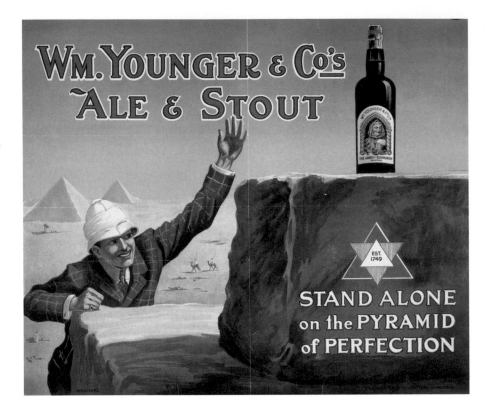

life above stairs, with a white cloth laid and all seated according to rank. Publications with advice about home-making, cooking and entertaining were still of great importance, such as Mrs Humphrey's *The Book of the Home*, which appeared in six volumes in 1909. Some were now aimed very specifically at households that did not keep a servant, such as *Woman's World* magazine, published from 1903.

Fascination with Ancient Egypt, which was to reach fever pitch with the opening of Tutankhamen's tomb in 1922, started in earnest in the Edwardian period as a result of a number of British archaeological discoveries. This particular find on one of the great pyramids, though, is not ancient and certainly not Egyptian.

Going out for tea or a fish supper

Although in the twenty-first century it is fashionable – as it was in much of the nineteenth – to meet friends or pass the time at a coffee shop, it was the tearoom that held sway during the intervening years. As early as 1864, the Aerated Bread Company (ABC), the London bakery that had pioneered new technologies in bread production, started a vogue for drinking

The Aerated Bread Company (ABC) cafe on Ludgate Hill, London is packed out in 1900. Such establishments, serving hot drinks and snacks, were respectable places for a modest bite out and for social encounters. The sign above the stairs reads 'Ladies' Coffee Room Downstairs', a venue in which women could rendezvous out of earshot of their menfolk and without adverse comment.

tea while out by deciding to serve the beverage to customers at one of their bread shops. The enterprise was a runaway success and other caterers followed suit; by the end of the century the tearoom was an established meeting place. In 1894 Joseph Lyons opened his first teashop in London's Piccadilly, and by 1909 had established the first Lyons Corner House, an institution that was to dominate city-centre tea drinking well into the twentieth century.

Lyons Corner Houses achieved a winning blend not just of teas but of atmospheres: the exteriors of the buildings were a light, modern white and gold while interiors were glamorous and faintly exciting; but at the same

time the style of service and eating was fully respectable. Huge spaces spanning several floors and with slightly overblown décor, hung with chandeliers, gave the air of a ballroom (and often orchestras were playing); yet the waitresses were smartly but austerely decked out in black uniforms, serving nothing more intoxicating than tea and cakes. The exceptional aspect of Lyons tearooms, and of other chains and individual establishments that followed the trend, was the comparative democracy, both of class and gender, of their customers. Men and women, or women together and unchaperoned, and from different social classes, were seen alongside each other at tea tables, eating and drinking from the same menu, waited on in the same way. J. Lyons and Company were catering pioneers, not least through this ability to blend the mildly exotic with the socially acceptable and the socially diverse. The Lyons formula also proved hugely

The tearooms of the London Coliseum theatre were designed in spectacular Arts and Crafts style, plus some Art Nouveau flourishes, by Frank Matcham in 1904. The vivid pea-green wall and floor colour is fashionably daring. Beautifully turned-out waitresses stand ready.

Waitresses at Kate Cranston's Willow Tea Rooms in Glasgow are exotically dressed, with beaded chokers and satin bow ties to complement Charles Rennie Mackintosh's avant-garde 1903 interior. His unique and innovative designs are seen in the stained glass partition and in the table supports.

popular at the Trocadero Restaurant, which the Lyons Company was to open in 1896 in Shaftesbury Avenue, London, complete with grand baroque interiors and grand Edwardian catering. More exclusive than the tearooms, but still catering for a wide clientele in its various restaurants and private dining rooms, the Trocadero was famous for its interior, particularly a ninety-foot-long frieze of Arthurian scenes and, from 1901, the vast stretch of the Long Bar – although this was for gentlemen only.

Smaller entrepreneurs had an eye for the commercial charms of tea taken in a chic interior, too. In Glasgow, Kate Cranston had grown up surrounded by talk of food and drink. Her father was a baker while her elder brother was a tea dealer who had started a small chain of no-frills teashops in the city at the end of the nineteenth century. Kate's particular genius was to recognize that customers would be attracted in greater numbers by something more striking than the purely functional: the environment in which they were to take their tea was crucial to the venture. She opened her first tearoom in 1878, splendidly decorated, and continued in the same way, commissioning innovative interior designers to produce tearooms in the Scottish Arts and Crafts style. Miss Cranston's Tea Rooms in various locations in Glasgow were a great success. Modern, unusual, equipped with men-only and women-only rooms as well as luncheon rooms where the sexes could respectably meet, they were a unique mix of high fashion, cleanliness and simple good tea and luncheon menus.

Kate Cranston's patronage of contemporary Scottish artists of the Arts and Crafts school was a significant boon to their careers and, most memorably, to that of Charles Rennie Mackintosh, who became involved with the

SIMPSON'S IN THE STRAND
The Famous Old English Dining House.

Telephone Nos.
4333
and
4334
Gerrard.

Telegraphic
Address:
"SIMPSONS,
STRAND,
LONDON."

VETERAN CARVERS AND SUPERINTENDENTS AT SIMPSON'S.
(The youngest of them has served there for over a quarter of a century.)

OPEN ON SUNDAYS FOR DINNERS FROM 6.0 P.M.

Manager, N. WHEELER.

design of her tearooms from 1897 and continued to work for her over the next twenty years. Mackintosh first provided wall murals in tearooms in Buchanan Street, then he moved on to design the furniture for those in Argyle Street. In 1903 Mackintosh started work on the Willow Tea Rooms in Sauchiehall Street, now – in collaboration with his wife Margaret MacDonald – having charge of the whole interior layout and design project. The Willow extended over three floors, with interlinking restaurants, the most spectacular of which was the Room de Luxe, glittering with leaded mirror friezes and silver-grey chairs of the now familiar but then rather extraordinary elongated Mackintosh form. The unique total design look of the Willow Tea Rooms meant that they became the most famous of Miss Cranston's catering empire, regularly visited and written about by the famous and infamous and hence the place to be seen in Glasgow.

The ordinary pleasures of eating a simple meal out, or taking one away, were dominated at the start of the twentieth century by small restaurants and shops, rather than by the plethora of street stalls that characterized the nineteenth-century food and drink trade. The pie man, even then under threat, and the street seller of fried fish laid out on newspaper with

A promotional postcard for Simpson's restaurant in the Strand, London glamorizes the 'veteran carvers' who supply the best Sunday roast. Carving was seen almost as an art form, certainly as an essential masculine accomplishment.

salt on the side that Henry Mayhew observed and described in such detail in 1851 had given way to the pie shop and, from about the 1860s or 1870s, the fish and chip shop. There are many claims from around Britain for the first fish and chip shop, from London to Lancashire, but the most frequently cited is for one opened in Bow in London's East End by a Joseph Malin in 1860.

The origins of the popularity of fried fish in Britain are also unclear, but the dish was an established element of Jewish cuisine and may have been adopted in Britain as a result of this influence. Certainly, Jewish recipes for deep-frying fish had appeared in a number of Victorian recipe books. The fashion was no doubt encouraged by the fact that fish had long been a comparatively cheap source of protein, so that many people had developed a taste for everything from whelks to herrings. The origin of the chip seems to be even more difficult to trace, some ascribing it to the north of England, some to French influences. But by the beginning of the twentieth century the British taste for the two, in combination with salt and vinegar, was well established and fish and chip shops have flourished ever since. The meal has even acquired the status of a national dish. Pie shops were numerous by the end of the nineteenth century and proliferated at the beginning of the twentieth, particularly in London. Typically, they sold hot meat pies with mashed potatoes and a bright green 'liquor', a sauce made of parsley, butter, flour and malt vinegar – and jellied eels, which are stewed eels in a spiced jelly.

Customers eat in and take away fish and chips from a supper bar in London's East End, in an engraving of 1892. The brisk trade shows the popularity of the meal a couple of decades after the opening of London's first fish and chip shop in about 1860.

158   Although these pleasures of eating tea or a fish or pie meal out were increasingly democratic for a span of middle- and working-class people, in Edwardian Britain there existed a chasm between the eating habits of a plutocrat and those of a poor labourer. There were many families in which only one good meal was eaten a day, and that in itself could be meagre, in a diet often still based on tea, bread and jam or dripping, potatoes and bacon. In poorer families meat was only eaten once a week, and for very many working-class people a chop or a kipper on a Sunday was a considerable treat. As in the nineteenth century, often the only place of escape and entertainment was a public house. Although an attempt to solve some of the problems of drink had led the authorities to make it more difficult to gain a liquor licence, there was still one pub for every three hundred people in the country. Statistics suggest that every Edwardian adult drank an average of six pints of beer a week, and there were thousands of prosecutions for drunkenness.

A poster of May 1911 advertises a commemorative beer brewed to celebrate the crowning of George V, seen in his ceremonial splendour with Queen Mary. Representatives of the British empire, in their national dress, snake around the new king and queen.

High society

At the opposite end of the Edwardian social scale it was a completely different story, one of conspicuous consumption on a scale compared to which much Victorian ostentation paled by comparison. Between 1890 and the First World War, London was the financial capital of the world. A new wealthy elite, either indigenous or passing through, had fully assimilated a sense of right to the privileges it could afford and its members did not fight shy of demonstrating their new status. Edward VII, a man notorious as a

The artist of this 1912 poster has fun with a bustle of fine gentlemen, who have, of course, all requested the same brand of whisky. The mirror on the wall illustrates a scene from behind the bar from the barmaid's point of view, and the doorway reveals yet more contented drinkers climbing the stairs.

bon viveur and womanizer, included in his social court the fast-living *nouveaux riches*, 'tradesmen' rather than aristocrats, including a Jewish elite of Rothschilds, Beits, Cassels and other such financiers. Edward VII's home and continental social whirl would take him yacht racing at Cowes, to Spa towns in Germany or Austria, deer stalking in Scotland, shooting at his house at Sandringham in Norfolk, to the French Riviera and to a round of

160 theatre, opera or music hall productions as part of the London season.

Social manners had propriety as their outer shell, but it could be as contrived as the styles of dress of the period, a cosmetic shield for inner indulgences and covert indiscretions. An Edwardian lady's appearance was one of a highly wrought artificiality that symbolizes this disguise of true natures, and the lengths that had to be gone to in order to maintain and demonstrate social standing. Her expensive clothes needed maintaining by her servants and were designed specifically for each type of occasion – the tea party, the dinner or the ball. Leisure time could be absorbed by the necessity of changing outfits several times a day, while the maid's time would certainly be absorbed in constructing hairstyles around wads of padding to achieve the desired 'big hair'. Delicate lace gowns could shroud steely personalities, and an air of respectability be maintained by the presence of a suitable hat, trimmed with ostrich feathers, which might have cost thousands of pounds at today's prices. Gentlemen were similarly trussed in costumes that observed a strict social code, according to the occasion. Edgar Jepson, in his *Memories of an Edwardian*, complains of the complexity of such dress:

> I had always resented the unreasonableness of men's clothes,
> especially their unreasonableness in the matter of buttons. No
> man can cover himself decently from the eyes of his fellows
> without buttoning over twenty buttons.

Such outward appearance was to be policed as a matter of priority. In E.M. Forster's 1908 novel *A Room with a View*, for example, the unaffected Lucy Honeychurch is tutored in these matters by her mother at a garden party shortly after Lucy's misguided engagement to the passionless Cecil:

Although the feel of this whisky poster is different from those that depict men in evening dress, the class associations persist. The men reaching out for the brand are travelling first class, and are officers in full military regalia.

Irish whiskey takes on a dreamy, almost surreal quality in this unusual poster of 1911. The man in the moon has a frighteningly realistic human hand, which stretches out from the clouds of a stormy night so that he can take a swig.

At tea a misfortune took place: a cup of coffee was upset over Lucy's figured silk, and though Lucy feigned indifference, her mother feigned nothing of the sort, but dragged her indoors to have the frock treated by a sympathetic maid.

Cecil is a stuffed shirt described by Forster as 'well educated, well endowed, and not deficient physically', but a man who 'remained in the grip of a certain devil whom the modern world knows as self-consciousness, and whom the medieval, with dimmer vision, worshipped as asceticism'. Luckily, Lucy has the modern nerve to escape the fate of marriage to Cecil, opting successfully for a bit of social mobility and marrying for love a man of the rising middle class.

Of course, indulgences revealed themselves in no small part through eating and drinking. Parties given at home offered elaborate ball suppers, sometimes followed later by yet more meat and sweet dishes to sustain the hungry dancers in the early hours of the morning. Fancy dress parties were particularly in vogue, such as that recounted by Jepson, which he attended dressed in Turkish garb. His wife and baby Selwyn came, too:

It was a good party, and there was a great deal of champagne, a drink which, in those simple days, always endeared our hosts to us, and about the middle of the party we brought the sleeping Selwyn from the bedroom and set him in the middle of the floor and danced round him. He did not wake up; we knew he would not; it was his sleeping time, and he slept. He was a good baby.

Picnics, their style pioneered by previous generations of Victorians, were enormously popular with the Edwardians. The problems of transport, of food and guests, were now largely overcome, and it was possible to picnic

162 in real style. Special recipes were created for the picnic occasion – potted cheese and potted pâtés – and new tablewares were required, such as a wicker 'sauce basket' to accommodate the bottles of relish to highlight the food. Picnickers could travel to locations by motor car, with necessary furniture and fittings stored in the boot. A folding luncheon tray, for example, rather like a butler's tray, was so much more elegant than scattering the food across a cloth on the ground. And if boating was on the agenda, a table to fit across a punt or a rowing boat could be brought along – unless there was a folding table already fitted to the boat in question. The picnic fashion was part of an Edwardian obsession with the benefits of fresh air, indulged in lighter interiors with larger windows thrown open, and typified a general tendency to eat outside whenever the climate allowed. A table could be taken outside and laid out with cloth and silver and glass in just the same way as it would be inside. Newly built, large

This imaginary car made of potted meats, jars of pickles and bottles of relish looks quaint, but represented a thoroughly modern form of transport in the first decade of the twentieth century. Preserved foods were by now big business, hence the slogan claiming brand pre-eminence.